BE
THE
LOVE

BE THE LOVE

A Woman's Journey from
Fear to Freedom

SARAH PROUT

ST. MARTIN'S
ESSENTIALS
NEW YORK

Published in the United States by St. Martin's Essentials, an imprint of St. Martin's Publishing Group

www.stmartins.com

Designed by Steven Seighman

The Library of Congress Cataloging-in-Publication Data is available upon request.

ISBN 978-1-250-90640-3 (trade paperback)

Our books may be purchased in bulk for promotional, educational, or business use. Please contact your local bookseller or the Macmillan Corporate and Premium Sales Department at 1-800-221-7945, extension 5442, or by email at MacmillanSpecialMarkets@macmillan.com.

First St. Martin's Essentials Trade Paperback Edition: 2023

10 9 8 7 6 5 4 3 2 1

For my children: Thomas Anthony,
Olivia Rose, Lulu Dawn, and Ava Moon.
Thank you for being here. I love you.

Contents

Introduction

Your Invitation

Welcome! I'd like to congratulate you for being here right now. I have a great deal of respect for your willingness to dive into themes that prompt self-discovery, healing, and personal growth—and I don't say that lightly. I see you. Amid the beautiful chaos of life, seeking to belong, navigating relationships, riding the wave of different emotions, and everything else that falls into the magnificent spectrum of being a human—I see you, and I honor you in this moment.

The book you are now holding in your hands or listening to in your ears is a book about LOVE and how to claim the hidden powers of your heart. It's a love letter and an invitation written specifically with you in mind. The theme of love is woven throughout the narrative like fine golden thread, and this is why it's so important to first define what love actually represents.

When you search for the word *love* in the dictionary it states that it's a verb (an action word) and that it's an intense feeling of deep affection. Simply put, love is a feeling felt in your heart. The reason it's so important to articulate this is because reality and relationships can be somewhat warped in the name of love. They can masquerade as attachment, control, and an endless thirst to seek love outside of oneself instead of from within. What you are about to read is the journey back to yourself and into your heart.

I have one very powerful intention for this book: I want you to be the love you wish to feel. Why? you might ask. Because the truth is that if you can't love yourself, honor yourself, and listen to your heart, then it becomes almost impossible to love others and to live a meaningful life filled with abundance, creativity, connection, and joy. Sadly, I know this firsthand because I have not felt worthy of love for most of my life. I was trapped in the seemingly endless cycle of seeking love, validation, and happiness from others instead of from within my own heart first. At times, I've felt disconnected from my own personal power, and this book documents how I made my way back to a space of clarity, alignment, intention, and confidence.

One of the most powerful techniques to help me get back on track was using affirmations in my moments when I couldn't love myself. Affirmations help to amplify the energy of your thoughts so that you can create a positive and empowering boost when you need it most. The word *affirmation* originates from the Latin *affirmare,* meaning "to make steady, strengthen or to fortify."

When you affirm belief in yourself and your desired outcome (either out loud, written down on paper, or silently in your mind), it leaves you feeling more confident, capable, and prepared for the experiences that unfold throughout life.

Alongside affirmations, I discovered these three potent core elements that can always return you to a state of love and of inspired action in your times of need. I call this the *Be the Love* philosophy: **feel, heal, and reveal.** The Be the Love philosophy is turning to your ability to guide your energy and wake yourself up to appreciation and the joy of being yourself. This philosophy is beautifully simple and effective when navigating throughout life.

1. **When you're hurt: FEEL.** Allow yourself to whole-heartedly explore your emotions and activate connection within your heart. You do this through first asking yourself how you feel, by choosing alignment, exploring truth, and being grounded in your body. Always check in to see if you are being defensive or reactive instead of open and curious. Feelings must be processed and honored to move forward in life.

2. **When you can identify a need for change: HEAL.** Embrace your imperfections, make peace with what is, and become more intentional in your life to take responsibility for your own emotional reactions and responses to people and experiences. This will contribute to your well-being and help you reclaim your happiness.

3. **When you open your heart to all possibilities: RE-VEAL.** Trust that you are always guided on your journey and have access to infinite wisdom and inspired ideas that will illuminate an empowered path forward. Your intuition will always be revealed when you lead with love from your heart.

Even if you choose to close the book at this point (and I sincerely hope that you don't), then it is my ultimate wish that you lean into just these three powerful elements with a sense of curiosity to understand how they have the power to radically transform every area of your life.

OUR JOURNEY BEGINS IN YOUR HEART

We begin with a call to your heart and set the powerful intention to create an emotionally safe space for our time together. We're going to accelerate, amplify, and expand your capacity to seek guidance and comfort within. What I call *emotional alchemy* is turning feelings and emotions into a more loving perspective, and it's like learning a whole new language. It can be really liberating to remember to rise above fear and embrace love in as many different situations as possible.

The heart has been represented as a symbol throughout history to remind humans of their capacity to transform, feel, and heal. Your heart itself, in your chest, holds tremendous intelligence as a guiding force to navigate your journey throughout life. In a way, it's like a compass of sorts. It can tell you if you're feeling good or feeling bad. It can open, and it can close. It can even break. The energy the heart contains is important feedback on a moment-by-moment basis to remind you of your own limitless potential if you're willing to tune in.

My intention here takes you on an emotional journey to transform your inner world first and foremost so that you can steady, strengthen, and fortify your emotional responses throughout life. This adventure begins within your heart for you to *Be the Love You Wish to Feel*. This means:

Be the change
Be the grace
Be the joy
Be the strength

Be the mirror
And, of course, Be the Love.

Love is the most important element because it can mean comfort, transformation, connection, medicine for the soul, a doorway to the divine, and so much more.

The exquisite subtleties that reside in this level of heart-based intention and awareness of embodying love will completely change the framework of how you live your life. To show you exactly how to do this, I'm going to be sharing with you some of the most vulnerable and life-changing emotional experiences that have unfolded in my own life over the last forty-two-plus years. In truth, it's been a really hard process for me to write this book because of the sheer level of emotional transparency required to share my story and map out my journey into tangible steps. It was such a great healing process for me as I hope reading these words will be for you.

My story to get here right now spans two marriages, ten pregnancies, at least five countries, several thousand buckets of tears, and an equal amount of excuses. There's also been a lot of love, laughter, adventure, and joy that has coexisted with the grief, the loss, and the tribulations. I've walked a challenging emotional path to get me to where I am today. It's a path that severely corroded my sense of self-esteem and the connection to understanding my true self. I'll be sharing so much more with you in great detail in the upcoming chapters of how I turned my pain into power. As one example, nothing is more heartbreaking than not having enough money to feed your children. I would feel helpless and hopeless on a daily basis. I went from living on welfare in 2009 as a single mother in Australia, to now running a successful million-dollar company in the United States. If I can learn how to manage my emotions and guide my energy in times of distress, then you can too. And it doesn't matter what has unfolded in your life to get you to where you are today. The key thing to remember is that if you live your life with self-love and emotional self-awareness as your North Star, then you will thrive. And I'm here to show you exactly how to do that.

Before we begin, please note that the themes in this book are not all sugarcoated with rainbow glitter; I am diving deep into topics such as domestic violence, recurrent miscarriage, addiction, guilt, depression, abuse, eating disorders, infidelity, and the many, many masks of shame. Sounds fun, right? Please keep reading. There will also be a lot of uplifting, happy, and beautiful stories here too. Stories that I hope inspire you to be the best version of yourself, master the art of deep self-care, and to not waste any time self-sabotaging and getting in your own way.

My guess is that you'll probably see yourself—or

other people you know—in many of my stories. There's also a possibility that you might not resonate with certain themes, and that's okay too. What I want you to remember is that I'm writing this book from my heart and from my own personal perspective. Many of the names have been changed in the book, but the intention is to only share stories that are mine to tell. Throughout this process, I have endeavored to be as inclusive as possible to make sure that this information is not only timeless but applies to anyone who holds a desire to make their life better in some way or another.

My stories time-hop too, which is why I've placed a date in the beginning of most sections so you can jump in the time machine with me and go on the journey.

WHY IS THE MESSAGE OF *BE THE LOVE* SO IMPORTANT AND NEEDED?

Over the years, I've learned to get more confident in saying yes to big and scary opportunities. In 2019, I partnered with Goalcast, a company that produces inspirational and often viral videos. In the video, I shared my story of surviving ten years of domestic violence during my first marriage. It was an incredible burden to carry that story for so many years and then to release it out into the world. I radically underestimated how it would highlight and reveal to me a further and deeper path of healing to take. The level of abuse that I endured went way beyond normal fighting between a husband and wife. These numerous moments of violence created long-term emotional scars I had no idea I was still carrying until the video went viral.

To my utter surprise, the video was viewed by over sixty million people on Facebook in the first year of its release. This is more humans than the population of Sweden, Hong Kong, and Australia combined! The energy of this level of attention reflected how many people are suffering and can relate to the dynamics of a dysfunctional relationship. It was also an opportunity for me to navigate how responsible I was being with my duty of care to the people that spent time connecting with me and learning from me online.

The message of the video was to Be the Love— three words I believed held power to inspire others. My intention was that this phrase would resonate with the viewers to love themselves more and to understand what is possible when you put your heart and mind into transforming your life emotionally after divorce, relationship breakdown, loss, or adversity. As you could imagine, this is very hard to communicate in a short, six-minute video, and I completely underestimated the unintended consequences of sharing this level of private pain with the world. Yes, the message resonated, but it still felt incomplete because I didn't get to explain the healing work required to transform my life. I also received thousands of comments from all over the world asking two very specific questions. The questions were simple but echoed my concerns that the video was only just scratching the surface of this very important topic: *"Sarah, how can I be the love? And where do I start?"*

It was a collective and heartfelt plea from so many people, predominantly women who felt tremendously stuck in their lives. They too were in various cycles of abusive relationships or struggling to move forward because they felt unworthy and powerless due to the pain of the past. What magnified this urgency was that they were assuming that I had some kind of answer for them—and at that exact point in time, in full transparency, I don't think I did. With some painful self-reflection and extremely raw self-assessment, I became aware that I was sharing my "rags-to-riches" story from a very surface-level place of victimhood instead of from the space of emotional empowerment. So I started on the journey of writing this book, and the first step was to live the philosophy day to day.

I had to walk the talk, embody the work, and take full responsibility for how I had shown up in my life to get to the place I am currently in. This is your invitation to do the same and the beginning of a powerful journey of emotional healing.

My promise to you is that if you practice the Be the Love philosophy (with my help!) in your own lives, you will:

- Transform your feelings of overwhelm, doubt, and fear into feelings of love, trust, faith, joy, connection, and meaning.

- Hone your skills of intuition so that you can determine if you are on the right path or unconsciously choosing to take a long way around. It's important to know the difference between your intuition and your anxiety.

- Dive into the concepts of deep self-care, finding your purpose, and how you can be more intentional with the way that you show up in the world.

You will achieve this by:

- Opening yourself up to your gut instinct, listening to your heart, and receiving messages from your higher self (or from God, the Divine, or the Universe).

- Setting powerful intentions about how you want to feel and what you desire to experience in every area of your life.

- Paying it forward to others with collective kindness exercises. There is a call-to-action exercise in each chapter to send good energy to others. This is based on the manifestation principle that the energy you put out there will return to you. Being the love is about making sure that being kind is a driving principle.

- Doing self-reflective exercises like visualizations, affirmations, and following specific journaling prompts that can be found at the end of each chapter. Taking the time for self-reflection can be one of the single most powerful healing tools that you can use to activate your heart. If you feel comfortable doing so, I would love you to share a photo of your journal and this book with our community on Instagram. Please tag me (@sarahprout) and use the hashtag #BeTheLove.

YOU ARE CORDIALLY INVITED

I want you to imagine in your mind's eye that you have been sent a beautiful envelope in the mail. The paper of the envelope is iridescent like the glow of an opal. A small heart has been hand-drawn in the top right-hand corner where the stamp should be. You intuitively know that the message inside the envelope has the potential to transform your entire life. The seal on the back has your initials embossed in a lilac-hued, metallic wax. As you break it open, the delicious scent of jasmine flowers is released. Inside, the card contains a message from your higher self—the core essence of your unique presence in this world.

> *You are cordially invited to celebrate the joy of being who you truly are. When you fully accept yourself is the moment you begin to heal and grow. Make peace with the present, empower your emotions, and the miraculous energy of love will be revealed in all areas of your life. Be the love you wish to feel, and it will change your world. Always remember you are worthy.*

Your next step is to RSVP to this invitation. There are three boxes to tick:

- ☐ *YES.* I am willing to graciously accept myself.
- ☐ *No, thank you.* I'm perfect. See you next lifetime.
- ☐ *Maybe.* I'm open to trying, but I'm unsure this will work because nothing else has.

I believe many of you will select *Maybe*, and that's perfectly okay. Being open to possibilities is in fact one of the best places to begin your journey truly objectively. Some of you will have a resounding and full-bodied *Yes* because you are ready and might have already done some personal development work, and you're committed to remembering that deep self-care requires ongoing maintenance. And for those of you that select *No,* then what would have to happen to turn it to a maybe? I'm being playful here, but reading a book titled *Be the Love* is not really the right time to go into shutdown mode. I really want you to attend this party to celebrate who you truly are. *You are worth celebrating.* I don't give two hoots who you are, who you think you are, what you have done, mistakes you have made, or reasons you believe that you are not worthy enough to experience the joy of being you. I'm here to invite you to celebrate the all-encompassing parts of you—even (and especially) the hidden parts that you would never want anyone to know about. We all have flaws, quirks, unique personality traits, and peculiar ways of doing things, and it's all totally acceptable as long as it's not harming anyone else. No amount of shame that is carried cannot be undone by the power of love and of emotional intelligence.

ARE YOU READY?

If you are brave and willing to examine your emotional patterns, I promise you that magic will happen. The next seven chapters of this book will radically shift your perspective. Along with the chapters are seven affirmations to embrace that will help you to find your path back to love when you might feel like you have lost your way a little bit.

Close your eyes for a moment. Take in a deep breath and say, "I am ready." Now imagine yourself being surrounded by the energy of unconditional love and infinite wisdom. When you feel it in your heart, even if it's just a tiny spark of a feeling, turn to the next page.

1

Believe in Your Own Magic

Close your eyes, breathe in deeply, exhale, and then say this affirmation: *I am worthy.*

You might feel a little silly doing this at first. You might also notice resistance and doubt rush to the fore-front of your mind, but the key point is to stick with it and witness how you feel in your heart. Over time, you will experience benefits such as boosted confidence and inner balance. Affirmations are one of the most pow-erful ways for you to believe in your own magic and manage feelings of self-worth. I often wonder when the exact moment was that I didn't feel good enough about myself for the very first time. I imagine there had to be a precise and finite event when I made the firm decision to question my value. My mother often quotes some-thing I said when my little sister was born in 1983:

"Wasn't I good enough for you, Mummy?"

My mother would often tell me that I was "overly emotional" and would experience the highest of highs and the lowest of lows. She was right. As a deeply empathetic child, I was toying with and internalizing the idea of worth before I truly even knew what it meant. Initially, I desperately wanted my mother to return Baby Henrietta to the hospital. I'd had three years and three months being the center of attention, and now this new-and-improved addition to our family orbit was stealing my spotlight. Of course, during our childhoods, we were the best of friends, with a healthy amount of sibling rivalry. This is probably a very familiar story for many of you, depending on the order you were born in your family.

The best thing about being raised by my parents was that there was always a lot of laughter, love, music, and art in our household. My parents were (and still are) highly creative and artistic, so they embodied the truest essence of creativity and entrepreneurialism even in the worst of times. I grew up in galleries and studios in Australia and New Zealand. At my father's watercolor exhibitions, my sister and I would be wearing cute matching dresses and were instructed to be on our best behavior, especially in front of the wealthy patrons. I would only speak when spoken to, and it was expected of me to always be polite to the customers— which was tough when sometimes they gave off an unsettling vibe. This was definitely setting the stage for me to become a people pleaser in adulthood and to question my worth. Having the responsibility of being "well behaved" placed on my young shoulders felt like quite a burden at times. It probably looked somewhat perfect from the outside, but in reality, it repressed my voice and trained me to place the needs of others above my own.

Behind closed gallery doors, my parents would often fight about money, fight to be right, and fight to be heard. Their primary objective was to wound one another with their words. Getting money into the household sometimes felt like it was more important than my well-being. When I was about seven years old, I would pray at night that they would get a divorce or make a lot of money because I wanted them to somehow find peace. I suffered terribly from anxiety because I didn't like them fighting so often. My anxiety manifested as nail-biting, recurring nightmares, and bedwetting—all classic signs that a child could be struggling emotionally. I held the fear and lack of worthiness in the pit of my stomach and at one point actively chose not to eat. I basically refused to nourish myself as a silent protest to hopefully one day have my anxiety managed or for the situation to change. It was a method and mode of control—something I had power over despite how out of control I felt. As a child, when you hear your parents fighting, you think it's your fault—which ultimately leaves you feeling even more powerless internally. What I didn't see or couldn't possibly understand back then is that there is a tremendous pressure that accompanies bringing money into a household to feed a family, being an entrepreneur, a self-employed artist, or even a parent, for that matter! The sheer level of self-belief and motivation required to thrive and survive while raising small humans is definitely not for the fainthearted. In time, I learned not to blame my parents for the rough patches experienced in my childhood. Instead, I chose to celebrate them for the incredibly resourceful and amazing people they are and the sacrifices they made along the way. I feel so blessed to have been raised by such creative and resourceful humans. Ultimately, my parents did the best job that they knew how to do— like most parents out there. To get to this point of resolution and deeply honoring my parents, I had to make the journey back to believing in my own magic rather than holding others responsible for my past, present, or future. Ironically enough, this required me taking a slight detour to first become exactly like my parents—not that I did that consciously. I became an entrepreneur who would fight with my spouse (in front of my children) and fight to be right. I dragged this cyclic baggage into my own two marriages, where it became as clear as day that I was sabotaging my own magic, instead of believing in it.

VULNERABILITY IS TRANSFORMATIVE

My lack of worthiness and pattern of toxic reactions meant that in my past I have been the abuser and also the abused. This is pretty shocking, right? Especially for a woman that has an inspirational viral video about surviving domestic violence. Please keep in mind that I do not make this statement lightly. It's actually really hard to admit this, but I know it's going to help a lot of people understand how lack of self-esteem grows in the shadows like mushrooms tend to flourish in the dark. It's important for me to take full responsibility and show you how I have formed the deepest of boundaries within my heart to ensure that certain lines are never crossed again. Some of these lines I didn't even really know existed until I got very emotionally raw with myself about the dynamics of mutual abuse in any relationship. It's no surprise that I had repressed anger issues when I'd spent decades placing other people's needs above my own. I knew that it was finally time to heal and to change my ways.

The pain that is created when you hurt someone you love manifests as such a heavy burden. I was pretty good at playing the victim role too and even better at not taking ownership of how I participated in the cycle of abuse. Most of the time, I never stopped to give it much thought. I always believed I was winning in some way when I played the blame game, making statements like this:

"It's your fault I feel this way!"
"You did this to me!"
"It's your responsibility to make me happy!"

When you make statements shifting blame onto another person, you hand over your magic. On a personal level, victimhood like this is a surefire way to corrode all connections with truth and harmony when you hold others accountable for how you feel. The good news is that when you can identify a cycle, you can break it and even reinvent it. Just like a farmer can look to the skies and know when a storm is brewing, you must learn how to identify your own emotional weather patterns and how to respond accordingly when you feel a wave of blame rising up within your heart.

1. **Activate your magic**—Stand back and give yourself permission to heal instead of permission to harm. Witnessing your emotions rising up in the present moment requires you to listen, pause, and then respond. This means getting really good at managing your own energy and knowing when it's time to step back and get some space.

2. **Change your beliefs**—You must hold the belief that lashing out at others is an expensive transaction that

drains your energy and is definitely not worth your time. Examining the way you react and respond to people, especially during an argument or a disagreement, helps you to become more self-aware. When you are violent and demanding with your communication, it's like drinking poison and expecting the other person to die. Affirm the belief that you are capable of cultivating peaceful skills for conflict resolution.

3. **Know your boundaries**—Being in attack mode is a sign that you have gone too far. I know this seems simplistic, but sometimes people don't sense that a line has been crossed until they have crossed it. The bull is out of the gate. When a wound gets triggered and activated, it's time to take a breath, a break, and self-soothe.

MAKE THIS YOUR MANTRA: THERE IS NO EXCUSE FOR ABUSE

One evening, I repeatedly (physically) pushed Sean, my husband. I then screamed at him to get out. Then I pleaded with him to stay when he packed his suitcase to go to a hotel for the night to get some space. My codependent tendencies were in full swing, and I was desperate for Sean to match the intensity of my energy.

He wouldn't and (understandably) was clearly disengaging to avoid being attacked any further. I called him names, told him he was a coward, blamed him for the state of our business and our life (we were having some problems), and continued to lash out like the tail of an agitated scorpion. I lost control emotionally. I wasn't taking a pause. I wasn't self-aware. I wasn't able to self-soothe. I was scrambling for him to make me feel better, or validated, or healed. It was like someone had unleashed the Hulk, and although I didn't turn green, my anger was like a tornado of fury. The shame that accompanies even writing these words leaves me feeling extremely saddened and disappointed in myself to this day.

I didn't know it at the time, but in the days that followed, this sobering and final deal-breaking violent outburst gave me three incredible gifts:

1. **The gift of FEELING:** No self-respecting person spits hateful and venomous words at a human they love. It boils down to this: people who are hurting also hurt others. I had to own it and learn how to process my emotions by allowing myself space and time to do this. I had to treat myself with the same gentleness, kindness, and compassion with which I would treat a small child. My inner child was not sure how to self-soothe without pushing the self-destruct button, so

I had to become hyperaware of my emotions and how I was processing them. Meditation and affirmations helped a lot to move through each moment, which is why I added them to each chapter of this book.

2. **The gift of HEALING:** If I behaved like this over and over again, Sean would probably (or should probably) leave me. The very real risk of this made me immediately seek to begin healing my trauma. I didn't want to hurt him. There was no way I was going to lose the love of my life. The stakes were too high, and I intuitively knew that I had been sweeping my issues under the rug and it was time to deal with them once and for all. The pain became severe enough for me to change, and I was ready and willing to do so.

3. **The gift of REVEALING:** When I made the decision to change my behavior, I knew there would be things that I would no longer tolerate in my life. When you make a brave decision to change and transform, the clarity that often accompanies the intention is really beautiful. The old energy that no longer serves you falls away to create space for the new. For the first time in my adult life, I had to embody the choice to react and respond consciously with my communication and from a space of love.

These three gifts are breakthroughs that I am proud to say have changed my life and were the foundation for the Be the Love philosophy. It hasn't been easy to confront these demons, but it has been totally worth it.

FEEL TO HEAL

I had to examine my feelings—like anger and rage—to explore the reasons why they kept appearing in my life. We all have access to our inner levels of wisdom when we remember to listen to our feelings. All it requires is taking time to pause and observe, rather than to instantly react. I truly believe it's not that feelings get hurt, it's that feelings don't have the space that they need to be understood, translated, and processed with compassion. We all have different rules and operating systems, and so when we find ourselves in a sacred union with another human being, it's no wonder that we either move toward togetherness or veer off the rails into separateness. I had something that I refer to as *slow simmer syndrome*. It's where all my unexpressed thoughts, self-criticisms, and irritations were building up in my heart like a pressure cooker ready to explode. As a remedy, my mentors helped me and encouraged me over the years to *tell the truth faster* instead of bottling it up. This means being willing to have difficult conversations *as they arise as feelings* so you can squish the monster while it's still tiny.

The reality is that most couples fight and argue at some point during their relationship, whether it's squabbling about division of housework or pleading for the toilet lid to remain closed. It's also very common for us to attract the perfect partners that bring our wounds to the surface to heal our emotional pain, especially when it comes to our levels of worthiness. Some of the most obvious ways our powerlessness manifests in conflict is to get defensive, withdraw, or even go into attack mode, which has obviously been my path and previous pattern.

For many years, I hid behind the excuse of entitlement to be emotionally distressed because of my toxic past. I stayed in an abusive relationship for ten years, I was raised by parents that I assumed had issues, I lived in poverty as a single mother, and I dealt with other abuses along the way. All these things changed who I was. I truly believed I was broken and that life was happening *to me* instead of *for me*.

There came a turning point where I began to question myself. Saying things like, *At what point does one say, "Enough is enough"? At what point is it time to be at peace with what is and move forward?* I had to get real with my feelings and face my inner demons with fearless strength to know that being vulnerable like this would help many people along the way. To do this, I knew it was time to stop pushing my feelings down with my addiction to food, to alcohol, to shopping, to being argumentative, or to any of the other things I would use to numb my experience. It was time to listen to my heart without distractions or self-perpetuated disturbances.

WHAT IS THE MESSAGE YOUR HEART IS TRYING TO TELL YOU?

Your heart is always giving you messages, and it's fun to think of it as your oldest and dearest friend. It was with you from the beginning of your life and will be there until the very end. When we trace back the patterns in our lives, it's often very clear to see a road map of ways that we have ignored the messages from our hearts. Smartphones, social media, apps, consuming excessive amounts of news, online shopping, and all the other ways we can tap out from the present moment are hindering the opportunities to create new pathways for healing in our hearts and minds. The main reason for this is because it's uncomfortable and of course painful to change. Our minds will do anything they can to avoid getting hurt. However, if things aren't working in your life with other people, then more than likely there is some profound space for healing to be done. And it begins with ownership of your emotions, being willing to do the work, and being open to trusting yourself.

WHEN YOU CAN TRUST YOURSELF, YOU CAN TRUST YOUR INSTINCTS

Here's a question for you. If someone told you a juicy secret and instructed you not to tell anyone else, could you keep that secret? If not, then remember this:

People that break trust usually do not trust themselves in various situations in their lives.

When you break trust, it usually results in feelings of guilt in your heart. It's that pang of guilt and feeling bad about something that is a key indicator of the edges of your boundaries and your levels of integrity. You know you have done something wrong, and that wrongness then manifests into feelings of shame that have no place to go but inward. This event then triggers a block in your ability to be intuitive and truly loving.

When you set clear boundaries in your life, you begin to see patterns of how much you value yourself, your time, and your energy. A method of starting to set healthy boundaries in your life is to make a pledge not to harm others and to always be a person driven by integrity. Try affirming these qualities in the following ways for yourself:

- I am trustworthy
- I am reliable

- I am honest
- I believe in my own magic

What I've understood over the years and more so recently is that learning how to Be the Love when you are on a healing journey to trust yourself is the ultimate remedy to pretty much anything that the Universe sends you as an obstacle, challenge, or emotional hurdle. Healing always begins with self-trust. It takes some training to set boundaries you will not cross, some serious practice, and some commitment to trying it out, but it's completely worth it to watch pain transform into power and fear morph into the comfort of faith. We can change the world when we first activate this magic within ourselves.

In the past, I felt so ashamed of the way I behaved—a personal development teacher falling into the cycle of abusive behavior and not trusting myself to keep my cool. Most people see shame as the final destination, but it's not. Shame is the invitation to be better, do better, and strive for breaking your own patterns of limited thinking.

The reason for this is because the nature of reality is woven together by choice points—very much like finding yourself at a fork in the road in each moment. You can choose your next actions, you can choose to respond in fear or love, abundance or scarcity, pain or even power. When you remember that you can choose to guide your energy and your emotions, then you are tapping into a space of pure love and infinite potential.

The answer? Be the Love.

Next time you enter into a space of disagreement with another human, ask yourself how you can Be the Love. Pause and choose how you want to spend your energy. It's not always easy, but it will allow you to watch the magic happen! The same rule applies when you feel ashamed of yourself in any way, choose again, and then again and again. You have and hold the power to navigate your emotional responses.

Sometimes one of the best ways to reverse engineer your beliefs and undo old ways of doing things is to glance back into your past—especially in some of your first memories of how you were able to manage certain social situations with your peers. Letting go sometimes requires looking back.

FIRST MEMORIES AND PATTERNS OF BELONGING

Melbourne, Australia, 1987

After story time, just before the end of the school day, the seven-year-old girls would all sit on the mat facing the teacher. Mrs. Nest would share homework assignments or allow someone to give out invitations to their birthday party. I was always aware that when you sit cross-legged in a school dress, you have to remember to make sure not to show your undies. Etiquette and self-consciousness seemed to be hardwired into my awareness. The uniform policy was very strict to ensure that the girls were always presentable to uphold the fine reputation of the school. I always felt like I was different from the other girls and something was wrong with me. Fitting in was something I tried to do but never felt like I could. I had a different accent from the other children since we moved from New Zealand to Australia when I was five. This was a talking point for the kids to say that I sounded weird and posh. And now this periodic invitation-giving process had my stomach feeling like I needed to poop, or puke, or both at the same time.

"Emily would like to share her birthday party invitations now," said Mrs. Nest.

I was so eager to feel chosen. The embarrassment of the previous week was still with me as a nervous presence. With all my seven-year-old enthusiasm, I had foolishly jumped out of my spot when I heard my name called. The only thing was that it was Sarah *B* and not Sarah *P*—an easy mistake to make. The whole class pointed their fingers and laughed at me, and I blushed like a beetroot. And I still didn't end up getting an invitation. Apparently, it was a fabulous event with miniature horses, epic goodie bags, and princess dresses for everyone to take home that they could keep.

I was weighing up the odds in my mind. I had a better chance of being invited to this party because Emily's parents were patrons of my dad's artwork.

Emily held the small stack of pink envelopes in her hands. There were over twenty girls in the classroom and only around fifteen invitations to be given out. There were people that were obviously going to go home disappointed and empty-handed. This odd invitation-giving ceremony felt like a really cruel way of separating the popular kids from the ones who weren't. It was inadvertently shaping belief systems of unworthiness that could potentially be carried for a lifetime. I didn't really like Emily anyway, with her high side ponytail hoisting up her hairline with a navy scrunchie. It had only been a few weeks since she had said to me in the playground, "You're so lucky to know me."

Her tone intimated that I was less important and influential than she was. Sadly, part of me agreed with her statement. Most of the parents of the girls in this prestigious Melbourne school were very wealthy—not that I understood what that meant back then, but I knew that money was important in some way. Their parents drove Range Rovers, and the kids had more toys, had bigger homes, and went on fancy trips to exotic locations. After my dad signed a bad business deal the very next year, we lost all our money and had to move. No more fancy school; most of our stuff was repossessed by the sheriff's department, and new shoes became a thing of the past. But for now, my world was hinged on the high hopes of being invited to this party.

"Amy, Emma, Felicity, Sophie . . ."

The girls got up to accept their invitations like they were at the Olympics getting a medal. I held my breath with anticipation. Time felt like it slowed down, and then when I least expected it, Emily called my name!

"Sarah Prout, you get to come to my party!" I jumped up, not caring about flashing my undies, and grabbed the invitation from her hand. It felt like winning something really important—like a golden ticket to visit a magical chocolate factory.

To the children who didn't get an invitation, there was no comfort from the teacher. This doesn't surprise me, since she allowed this kind of ceremony to occur quite frequently. I'm sure it had something to do with the mindset of society being a little different back in 1987. I so desperately wanted to belong, to feel chosen, to feel accepted.

This carried on into my adult life as well—more specifically when my ex-husband asked me to marry him when I was only twenty.

I said yes because I wanted to feel chosen. I should have said no.

I see so many women in the seven-year-old Sarah wanting to be accepted and the twenty-year-old Sarah who should have listened to her gut. And if I could tell my seven-year-old self anything now, it would be that life doesn't give you a fairy tale; you have to create it yourself by believing in your own magic and trusting that you are enough. I should have listened to my heart.

You'll see that throughout this book, I have intentionally referenced my relationships, crushes, or experiences with other boys and men. I did this to illustrate the cycle of seeking safety and approval, so you'll definitely see how this pattern was mapped out in my life thus far as a lesson. As humans, no matter our gender or sexual orientation, our soulful intention is that we want to feel connected to other people on a heart-to-heart level. We have a desire to share our lives. But sadly, sometimes we can hand over our magic and our personal power just for the sake of feeling like we belong.

When it comes to early child development, it's often said that the most crucial and critical milestones in a child's life occur by the age of seven. Apparently, the great Greek philosopher Aristotle once said, "Give me a child until he is seven, and I will show you the man."

The reality for many of us is that the ride from zero to seven years old might not have been ideal, but we begin to rewire and rewrite our experiences by examining our beliefs. These dangerous ripples of seeking approval were still with me into early adulthood, and I had no idea of the toll they were taking on me.

My Sense of Worthiness

When I was in my early twenties, my ex and I visited the seaside village of Burton Bradstock, in Dorset, England. It's positioned on what's called the Jurassic Coast because the site spans 185 million years of geological history. The cliffs are spectacular and look like ancient cathedral walls, holding wisdom and knowledge of the ages in each naturally etched piece of rock. As we drove along the coast, there were derelict houses that were clearly about to fall into the ocean. They looked like wobbly teeth about to fall out of a child's mouth. These homes were perched with such fragility on the rock face, unable to maintain the foundations on which they were built. I felt an odd sense of kinship with these uninhabitable homes—the lives they had once housed and the stories their faded walls could tell. This fondness and awareness didn't truly make sense to me until nearly two decades later as I'm writing this book and discovered that my ancestors lived there hundreds of years ago.

Just like coastal erosion where the cliffs experience the repetitive impact from waves, currents, tides, ice, storms, and the persistent nature of time, I realized how

I had lost connection with my true self for many years before I could identify that it had happened. My sense of worthiness was the house about to fall into the sea, my soul was the cliffs that were sculpted by the seasons, and my heart was the ocean—ever changing with the tide of emotional possibility. At some point, I forgot my power and lost control of the reins completely in body, mind, and spirit.

My lack of worthiness detoured and deflected its importance like a shape-shifting creature. I made my happiness dependent on the external world and the actions of others around me.

Your Body Is Not Your Worth

Just like you shouldn't build a house on sand (for obvious reasons), you can't expect to build healthy self-esteem on a foundation of self-loathing.

What is that? Is that cellulite?

It was 2002 or thereabouts. I was sitting on the floor with my legs crossed, drinking a cup of green tea and reading a magazine. I was wearing shorts, and for the first time ever in my young adult life, I could feel dimpled skin on my thighs when I would run my hand over my leg. I'd never noticed it before, and then it was just like an alarm of awareness was activated and set off in my mind. My thigh felt like the rippled texture of an orange peel—lumpy and squishy at the same time.

All of a sudden, I started seeing articles everywhere on how to get rid of cellulite: how to minimize it, how to cover it up, and, dangerously, how to restrict your diet so that it might go away once and for all. But nowhere was stating how to just love it, embrace it, and accept it because it's normal and almost 98 percent of women have it. I didn't even realize back then that I could either choose the path of shame and follow the herd mentality or choose the path of radical self-acceptance and set myself free. I was shaping my beliefs of who I was in the world based on what the media and advertising campaigns were guiding me to assume. This was a pattern for me, holding my value in the opinions of others. It was also the ripple effect (pun intended) of generations of women before me who never felt as if they were good enough or measured up to notions of perfection.

Dare to Compare

What I interpreted in my mind after discovering my newfound cellulite was that there was just another item to add to the ever-growing laundry list of things that were wrong with me. I identified the dimpled skin as bad, ugly, and unsightly—which translated into me *feeling* bad, ugly, and unsightly. I felt broken and not worthy, and I was definitely going to throw out every single pair of shorts that I owned. It is an extremely dangerous pattern to start believing you are broken because you don't measure up to an unrealistic physical standard.

Back then, I really just wanted to be normal. To this day, I really wish that I hadn't overplucked my eyebrows in the late '90s, because I would have saved a gazillion dollars on eyebrow pencils over the last few decades! Jokes aside, though, it's a powerful reminder not to make permanent decisions based on temporary trends or feelings. The beauty of life is that you grow and evolve over time. But again, let's be brave and real with one another. Even the most confident woman doubts herself from time to time and questions her worthiness. Sometimes we even change who we are just to fit in. We want to belong, to express ourselves authentically, and ultimately to feel loved.

What I've discovered is that there is a tiny cartoon devil that lives on the shoulders of most women—that is, until they realize that it has no true influence over them whatsoever. We set powerful intentions to live our best lives, be the best versions of ourselves, attract amazing opportunities, and be great mothers, lovers, present friends, and everything we need to be for everyone else but ourselves. The tiny cartoon devil then whispers gently into your ear like clockwork when the doubt rises up: *"Who do you think you are to want more for yourself? You're not good enough. Remember, you have cellulite."*

As the momentum of my self-loathing was quickly

gaining speed, I was just twenty-two, I had a six-month-old son, and I didn't own a single pair of shorts. I lived in Melbourne, Australia, and my daily routine was to keep our house clean, buy groceries, cook the meals, watch *Days of Our Lives* at midday, and care for the baby when my husband was at work from nine to five. If I filled out a form that needed me to state my occupation, it was *housewife*. This title wasn't what I wanted for myself. At twenty-two, I still didn't really know what I wanted to be when I grew up, but I knew it had to be something creative, exciting, or artistic like a movie screenwriter, a prolific painter, a bestselling author, or the owner of a successful company. Being a high achiever was a way that I could receive love. Actually, I still don't fully know how this pattern manifested in my life, but I'm sure it will be revealed in time.

And as for the housewife comment, keep in mind that for some people, being a housewife or househusband is their dream. If this is you, then I 100 percent support you. I've always known that I am a creative entrepreneur to the core of my soul—just like my parents. I'd been holding big dreams in my heart since I was about five years old to earn a sustainable living from my chosen art form. However, after I met my first husband, my life took a little detour into domestic duties, domestic bliss, and occasional domestic violence.

Twenty-two-year-old me knew nothing about caring

for myself, let alone another tiny human who quickly became my reason for living. My body was still recovering, even months later, from a thirty-four-hour-long labor that required seventeen stitches in my nether regions and the oh-so-necessary purchase of a hemorrhoid cushion.

My stomach muscles separated during the pregnancy and left me with a crumpled bag of skin on my belly. It sometimes felt like it could flap in the wind like a bedsheet pegged to a clothesline. I would literally have to tuck the apron of skin into my pants to hide it. Just days after the birth of my son, I was invited to a group physical therapy session for other new mothers in the maternity ward. We sat in a circle, and the therapist was asking us to watch out for a condition called *diastasis recti*—the partial or complete separation of the "six-pack" muscles, which meet at the midline of your stomach. If there has been a separation, you can feel it with your fingers. This lady knew it had happened to me, so she decided to use me as an example of a worst-case scenario. *Lucky me, here comes the shame.*

"Let's look at Jane's stomach. Hers will be flat; she'll be back in a bikini and beautiful in no time. This is Sarah's. You can see the separation here, and no amount of sit-ups will repair the damage and these unsightly wrinkles."

I was mortified. I felt ashamed. In fact, it was a

shame that I would carry with me, and tuck into my pants, for nearly eighteen years. I allowed this woman's lack of sensitivity to influence how I felt about my body for nearly two decades. In this three-minute (or less) moment of comparison, I handed my power over because I lacked the maturity not to take it so personally. Are you starting to see the pattern here? This is where it became easier to manifest my shame into victimhood, rather than just accepting myself fully. In that moment, if I'd had the maturity to do so, I should have focused my attention on gratitude and appreciation. I should have trusted that it was not this woman's intention to insult me or to create harm but an invitation for me to own my power. I can honestly tell you I would have gladly had the floppiest stomach on the planet if it meant that I could become a mother to my son.

However, during this time, I remember I got obsessed with body comparisons. I would see other women my age on TV shows, or in the movies, and wonder why their jeans fit them so perfectly and mine would leave me with a muffin top spilling over the sides. There was also another round of pernicious articles that grabbed my attention in glossy magazines too. They had headlines such as "Lose the Baby Weight Fast" and "Get Your Body Back After Baby." Remember, this was in the days before mainstream media outlets merged with the World Wide Web. Instead of scrolling social media feeds for headlines, I would scan the magazine stands at the grocery checkout to find out what Paris Hilton eats in a day to stay so slim.

I remember at that time, the famous supermodel Cindy Crawford had her baby girl just a few days after I gave birth. When I would shop for groceries, I would buy the magazine just because she was in it so I could see how her body was shrinking back after giving birth, and yet I felt mine was still gross, unsightly, and wobbly.

It was like a slow and silent competition in my mind that I could never win. I was comparing myself with highly edited, carefully curated, airbrushed examples of other humans. These celebrities probably had their own garden varieties of insecurities too. I would flip through the pages of these magazines and see Cindy Crawford spotted on a beach, in a bikini, having so much fun in a tropical location. And as I was reading about her, I was using it as an excuse to feel bad about myself. Little did I know that I was robbing my infant son of precious bonding time that he needed from me because I was so trapped in the prison of my own mind.

Comparison is not only the thief of joy; it is also the thief of precious time you can't get back again.

My Body Obsession Was an Echo of Recent Trauma

The previous year, before I had given birth to my son in 2001, had been one of the worst of my life. I was only twenty years old, and I'd lost my first pregnancy at around sixteen weeks due to a sudden miscarriage. My belly was just starting to show, and I was excited to start buying maternity clothes. I actually blamed myself for taking cold and flu tablets before I knew I was expecting. This was the main reason I thought that the baby's heartbeat had stopped and that it was all my fault. I didn't process the grief of that loss before getting pregnant again within just a few short months. When I made the sixteen-week mark, which felt painfully familiar, I was then physically assaulted by my fiancé. We had a violent argument where he backed me into a bathroom towel rail and repeatedly punched me in the arm. Knuckles tend to leave very distinct marks that are hard to hide. The bruise was so large that it spanned the length of my shoulder to my elbow. I didn't call the police, or my parents, or my friends. So what did I do? I chose to marry him only weeks later because everything was planned and I didn't want to disappoint our guests. I stayed because I didn't believe I had any other option. I was going to do whatever it took to take care of my son. I had a pregnant belly, bruises on my arms on my wedding day, and a corroded sense of self-worth. Even though he hurt me and I hurt him—we loved each other. But love is not supposed to hurt like this, and it's definitely not the best way to bring a child into the world.

The cycle of self-loathing and guilt seemed never-ending. After my baby was born, I suffered from un-diagnosed postpartum depression, which disconnected me even further from the beautiful gift of human life that I had just brought into the world. It was no won-der that I turned my attention to hating my cellulite instead of facing the reality that I really needed some emotional and mental health support to take control of my life.

I felt powerless, stuck, and empty because I was, and I had felt like this for so many years. Somewhere along the way, I allowed myself to believe that anything less than "perfect" wasn't acceptable. Now I realize, many years later, that there is tremendous beauty and strength in the imperfections. Dimples, wrinkles, scars, blem-ishes, stretch marks, crooked teeth, moles, and even cellulite aren't true measures of your worthiness. It's an invitation to see beyond the illusionary emphasis on outward appearances. And it all begins with setting the intention to change your mindset and to make the conscious choice to nourish and honor your temple.

BE GENTLE ON YOURSELF

In society, there seem to be these impossible standards that encourage women to compare themselves to others and then to buy into the remedy that could potentially up-level their feelings of being enough. It's like dangling a carrot in front of a donkey that's stuck on a hamster wheel—an endless maze of targeted advertising to navigate.

"If you lose weight, you'll feel happy, so buy this detox tea."

"If you look younger, then you'll find a man, so buy this anti-wrinkle, anti-aging face cream."

If you pair being exposed to advertising like this with not having enough support or space to process your trauma or emotions, then it becomes almost impossible to rise above the vicious cycle of self-rejection.

The subconscious impact of comparing yourself to others, or comparing your journey to someone else's, is radically underestimated in terms of how it affects your levels of self-esteem. Your insecurities and greatest fears are marketed directly to you by companies so you'll make a purchase. People that are vulnerable and don't feel very good about themselves make the best customers. So if unrealistic standards of "perfection" are set, then it's a super-easy and profitable sale. Sadly, the collateral damage is our self-esteem, and we don't even realize it as we part with our money. Unless you live under a rock, on a mountaintop, or in outer space, it is virtually impossible not to be exposed to the potentially damaging messages. *So what is one to do? What is one to do when the walls of an undesirable reality are closing in around them everywhere they turn?*

THE REMEDY IS SELF-AWARENESS

If you want to remove yourself from the cycle of comparison, then you must stop comparing yourself to others. Switch off. Unplug. Choose again. Unfollow. Block. Strengthen your awareness so that when you do see advertisements that are targeted to your fears, you see them for what they are. It is an opportunity for you to remember your power and believe in your own magic.

It's imperative to stay grounded and live your core values. Core values are the ways in which we conduct ourselves throughout life and the elements we hold dear to our hearts. The key to discovering these values is to look at the areas of your life that bring you joy and allow you to feel connected to your true potential.

- What do you love to do?
- How can you get swept away in an activity that makes you lose your sense of time?
- What makes you light up from within and/or makes you laugh until you are out of breath?

These are all clues to strengthen your sense of self-awareness in a world of illusions and distractions that want you to forget that you are way more than just a meat-suit inhabiting this physical reality. In a toxic relationship—or any relationship, for that matter—it's equally as easy to lose yourself and forget who you truly are if you are not vigilant and mindful. Abuse, previous trauma, loss, adversity, and lack of contentment in one's life can warp perception of what's real. Once you remember that you can step out of the illusion into a new world of awareness, then the beauty and fulfillment in your life will begin to gain momentum.

EMBRACE YOUR UNIQUENESS

We all have a frequency, or what I call a *signature energy pattern*, that rings true in our hearts. I'll be exploring this further in chapter 7 of this book. When you hear a song you love, when you read a piece of writing that resonates at the right time—it can be blissful. As humans, we are attracted to different things that represent who we are at a soul level. If you're not sure where to begin to identify what makes you unique, then try journaling or look online for public figures that inspire you in some way. This usually happens quite naturally and organically anyway based on your likes and dislikes. Everything from your taste in music to your preferred genre of movies—your uniqueness is often reflected back to you by what you find interest in.

I embrace my uniqueness through my writing, art, making people laugh, flowers, spending time in nature, my passion for manifestation, and finding things funny. I truly believe that life is a divine comedy. Laughter is like meditation. Each day, I make time to do things that I love to do—like sitting outside and looking up at the stars, or even making sure that I have new orchids in my house to brighten up a room. Hearing my children laugh and giggle also feeds my soul—knowing that they feel happy makes me happy too. I need to experience these anchoring moments of awareness so that I can keep my attention on the present moment and not lapse into old patterns of self-sabotage.

As soon as I feel myself comparing who I am to someone else (especially in social situations), I can either spiral into my pattern of negative thoughts or I can choose to remember the truth. I am unique, you are unique. Embrace your quirks, believe in your own magic, follow your heart, and you'll feel more empowered.

The sooner you learn how to embrace what you have, the sooner you'll make the journey out of your head and into your heart. I can guarantee you that there is someone out there in the world that would love to trade places with you in an instant. The things you dislike about yourself are what someone is probably praying for or wanting to manifest right now.

The power of embracing your own uniqueness is the key to your freedom. You must always celebrate what you have and do the best you can with it. This will radically impact the levels of joy and meaning that you experience in your life.

Collective Kindness Exercise 1

Make it your mission that within the next twenty-four hours you will give someone a genuine compliment. This helps to boost the confidence of others and is a really nice thing to do. Make someone's day by being the love.

THINGS THAT HELPED ME TO BELIEVE IN MY OWN MAGIC

1. **I took responsibility for my emotions:** One of the biggest game changers for me was to create a pause (or a moment of mindfulness) before instantly reacting

emotionally. I call this the magical space between intention and reaction. It's your feelings and your emotions that manifest your reality.

2. **I stopped comparing myself to others:** It was pretty intense when I was in my early twenties and I spent so much time trapped in a cycle of comparing my body to other women's bodies. As my business grew (in my thirties), I started to compare levels of success with others too. It was the same limited thinking keeping me stuck in a cycle. Every time I feel this way now, which still happens from time to time, I shift my focus back to gratitude, perspective, and celebrating key milestones. Everyone is on different time frames and on their own journey, and that is our cue to remember that comparison is the thief of joy.

3. **I learned how to show myself compassion:** After all the years of believing that I was not good enough and also dealing with the ridiculously high standard I always kept myself accountable to, I began to get curious as to how I could allow myself space to authentically process my emotions. Sadness, anxiety, and powerlessness would drop by for a cup of tea with my heart. I'd sit with them for a while in a space of nonjudgment and curiosity. When I felt the time was right, I'd give them a hug and then send them on their merry way. By viewing emotions as fluid feelings that would pass through like a storm, I began to see

the process of witnessing this energy as a great act of self-compassion.

4. **I became devoted to leading by example for the sake of my children:** As the mother of three daughters, I never want them to hear me speaking badly about my body in case they start feeling bad about theirs. The seed of unworthiness can grow faster than bamboo, so I'm blocking all the entry points of doubt. This is my duty of care.

5. **I started using affirmations:** One of the most powerful ways to guide your energy is through the process of repetition to imprint positive beliefs on your subconscious mind. There are countless messages being seeded into your brain on a moment-by-moment basis. When you choose to actively participate in what gets into your "mind palace," then you become more aware of how to stand guard at the doorway to your thoughts.

THE POWER OF THE PEN

Are you one of those people that loves to buy a new journal or gets super-excited when you buy a new pack of highlighters? I am a total stationery nerd and a paper lover. I love the potential that a blank piece of paper holds to change your life.

Whether you're setting powerful intentions, list-
ing out things to be grateful for, or venting your
frustrations—writing in a journal has numerous benefits. In fact, it may sound a little bit far-fetched, but a
2013 study* found that 76 percent of people who spend
at least twenty minutes writing about their thoughts
and feelings for a minimum of three days before a
medical biopsy were fully healed just eleven days after
the procedure. It was found that 58 percent of adults
(the control group) had not fully recovered.

Journaling is incredible for self-care and self-
reflection. I have included these theme-specific journaling prompts at the end of each chapter so you can
embrace the Be the Love philosophy or technology (if
you will) of feel, heal, and reveal. I sometimes call it
technology because it's a metaphor for you to download
this information and install it in your own operating
system (your heart). This happens when you have a fully
immersive experience in aligning with your thoughts
and feelings. The most important thing to remember
is that you should date your entries so you can review
them later, and don't hold yourself back from the flow

---

* Koschwanez, Heidi E., Ngaire Kerse, Margot Darragh, Paul Jarrett,
Roger J. Booth, and Elizabeth Broadbent. 2013. "Expressive Writing and Wound Healing in Older Adults: A Randomized Controlled
Trial." *Psychosomatic Medicine* 75, no. 6: 581–90. https://pubmed.ncbi
.nlm.nih.gov/23804013/.

of your responses. Create a safe space of nonjudgment. If you need any specific ideas of where to buy a beautiful journal, please visit SarahProut.com.

Are you ready? Here we go . . .

JOURNAL PROMPTS: Be the Love and Believe in Your Own Magic

FEEL: What are three things that you love and appreciate about yourself? What are three things that you love and appreciate about someone else? What are four feelings that you have experienced in the last seven days and why?

_____

_____

_____

_____

HEAL: What are the ways in your life that you've had to be brave? What were some defining moments that required inner strength? How have you blamed others for how you feel?

_____

_____

_____

REVEAL: Where do you see yourself in ten years? How will embracing your own magic change and transform your life? What change would you like to see in society or the world in the next ten years?

_____

_____

_____

2

You Are the Oracle

Close your eyes, breathe in deeply, exhale, and then say this affirmation: *I am intuitive.*

Everyone has intuitive powers. Whether they show up for you as a gut feeling or a little whisper, it's helpful to pay attention to the signs and messages we are being sent so that we can work with that information to create a more inspired path for ourselves.

I once went to get out of the passenger side of the car because there was nowhere to park during school pickup time to collect my children. Sean pulled to the side of the road, and just as I was about to jump out, a voice in my head said, *NO!*

I thought it was very strange, and so I paused before opening the door. During this split-second intuitive message, a school bus was speeding by and would have hit and killed me instantly had I left a moment earlier.

I feel so grateful to have paused and listened to the voice that stopped me from being harmed. To this day, it's hard to know whether it was a message from my higher self (my intuition), an angel, or a spirit guide— what I do know is that the message was delivered with perfect timing.

Another one of the ways my intuition illuminated a path forward in my life over the years is through dreams like this one:

A two-year-old boy sat cross-legged in the lotus pose on the floor of a barn. He looked like a cherub with blond curly hair. He had round and full cheeks as if he were painted by the great master Sandro Botticelli himself in the 1480s. The child seemed fully aware of his surroundings as he sat with a straight back on a pile of golden straw.

"See you when I'm ready to be born, Mummy," the boy said to me directly in a clear British accent. And then I woke up.

It was a school day, so I was eating breakfast before dashing out the door. I quickly told my mother about the dream I'd had, to which she said, "Sarah Prout, you are only sixteen years old, and I'm putting you immediately on birth control pills!"

This brash statement spoke deeply to my mother's faith in the prophetic nature of the dream world. She was always wired for superstition, which meant responding intuitively first and then asking questions later. Not that it was any of her business, but I hadn't even had sex for the first time yet. Furthermore, I had no intention of becoming a mother. I regularly drank cask wine (which we called "Two-Buck Chuck" back in the day) on the weekends with my friends because we were still deeply mourning the death of the late grunge icon Kurt Cobain. I rode a skateboard that had fluorescent-pink wheels, and I dressed up like Courtney Love. I wore baby-doll dresses, white tights, patent leather Mary Jane shoes, and smeared red lipstick. I wanted so badly to be a punk rock chick. The mid-'90s were all about the spirit of punk rock and grunge for me. My friend Kasey and I bought electric guitars and loved the idea of starting our own girl band, but it never happened. We spent so much time being rebellious, and it was incredibly fun. I used to steal my parents' cigarettes and alcohol, ditch school very regularly, and lie about my whereabouts. This was mainly due to being bored—a feeling I was never allowed to express as a child. My grandmother told me that being bored meant you had too much time on your hands. Perhaps she was right.

One day, Kasey and I decided to make a giant batch of fake vomit and deliver it to the mailboxes of the popular high school cheerleader–type girls we knew and hated in the local area. We mixed up cans of dog food, cheap aftershave, corn flakes, meat, milk, and anything that would help to make the most revolting, pungent, super-stinky concoction of chunder imaginable. We went on a long walk armed with trash bags of this faux puke. At each stop we made, we left a printed-out message that read, *Have the Vomit Fairies visited your house yet?*

And then I did something ridiculously stupid. I poured the leftover mixture into a community mailbox. A shopkeeper saw me do it and started to run after us, and we bolted down the street as fast as we could. It was nighttime, and we were wearing dark clothes, so, thankfully, we managed to get away. It could have been really bad if I'd gotten caught. In my mind at the time, I felt justified to do it. I felt entitled to pour fake vomit into at least three or four cheerleaders' mailboxes. What would their parents have thought? What was I really trying to express? Why did I hate these girls so much for being "normal" and "perfect"?

I had always held a deep knowing in my heart that I would never be a cheerleader type of girl (to be clear, not that there's anything wrong with that) that conformed to society's expectations of so-called perfection. I was never going to be the popular girl in school, let's put it that way. In Australia, instead of having a high school prom, we had something called a *debutante ball* where at sixteen years old you get presented to society. It was a clear *no thank you*. If I had to classify myself as anything, I was a wannabe punk rock chick with a chip on her shoulder and a heart that just wanted to find love or at least find validation from a boy. I would do love spells that I read about in magazines. I would practice visualization techniques and even speak to the Universe to send me a boyfriend. Little did I know that seeking to love a boy instead of loving myself first was a dangerous trap to fall into.

Throughout this time from age sixteen to eighteen, I kept thinking occasionally about my dream of the angel baby sitting cross-legged in a barn. It stuck in my consciousness with a feeling I just couldn't shake.

To my surprise, it was only around five years later that I held this baby in my arms. I'd grown up a lot, cleaned up my act (albeit on a very superficial level), and discovered deep, unconditional love for this child. His father had the same British accent. And when my son was two years old, he had round and full cheeks and golden curly hair just like in the dream. Here's the question I often ask myself: Did I create and manifest my experience based on the information in my dream, or did I tap into a glimpse of my predestined future? Did my son's soul send me a message, or did I manifest his form based on the data I collected from my dreamscape? I'm not sure I will ever know. What I do know is that there is a beautiful dance between divine order and the law of attraction. It's where your intuitive faculties intersect with the cocreation of your reality.

Simply put, energy creates matter. It always has, and it always will. The creative potential of this level of awareness is that every emotion you feel contributes to the energetic outcome of your future. Energy first (emotions) and then outcome second (manifestation). In each moment, you can either choose fear, or you can choose love, and it's in this distinction that your intuition is birthed.

SEEKING ANSWERS IN A WORLD OF DISTRACTIONS

Intuition is the ability to decipher energetic information, but many people haven't yet learned how because of the sheer volume of it presented to them on a daily basis. There is a slow and steady infusion of fear into society that has gradually disconnected many of us from our natural and innate levels of intuition. Ongoing exposure to fear can dull our sparkle just a little more each and every day, and we don't remember our capacity to rise above it. Many people don't even realize that it's happening. Our intuitive superpowers can become dull like a blunt ax or washed out like a faded old T-shirt. I'm defining *infusion of fear* here as a repeated, internalized emotional response to information placed into social media platforms, media outlets, ads, and news agencies that more often than not seeds the energy of concern. Simply put, the more you spend time worrying about the future, or being targeted to not feel very good about yourself, the more you distance yourself from your intuitive gifts. If you're online in any way, it's safe to assume you're in somewhat of an information bubble. I see this seeding of fear and limited thinking as the us-versus-them perspective that holds the intention to divide and conquer. For what reason, I'm not sure we'll ever know. I've witnessed dozens of people who believe in "light and love" that will swiftly block, unfriend, cancel, or unfollow if you hold a difference of opinion. This isn't unity. This is something known as *spiritual bypassing* that can tamper with your intuition like learning to run before you can crawl. I'll explore this more later in the chapter.

The problem with only believing what is in your bubble is that many people will believe everything they read and will respond without doing their due diligence to verify sources, going straight to the source, or understanding that the information can be spun and skewed with specific agendas to create division or to profit from fear. We become biased to the information bubbles we tune in to on a regular basis. However, intuition works differently, and there's a way to splinter yourself out of the information superhighway of agendas to seek clarity and empower your psychic centers instead of getting overwhelmed if you are willing to take an unbiased look.

The remedy for viewing the world in turmoil is to embody the Be the Love philosophy, because I truly believe it can shift some of the world's problems when we embrace more mindfulness, sacredness, and integrity into our day-to-day activities. This, in turn, helps to clear a path for greater levels of intuition.

Stand back (away from the news feed and your screen) and ask yourself these three questions when feeling emotionally charged by information you are presented with:

1. How can I raise my vibration and steady my energy to stay informed but detached?
2. Is it possible that this is not true?
3. How can I remain as loving as possible and honor the belief systems of others?

Fear as an energetic force will warp your perception of reality like standing in a house of mirrors. However, intuition is the difference between thinking you know and *knowing* you know. It's being aware of the fear and the love and the power each perspective holds to create the future. This level of discernment can only be present when you are able to stand aside from what you think is right or wrong or what your ego wants to assume.

We're all born with intuitive gifts, such as being empathetic or having vivid dreams or hunches as to how a particular situation will unfold. One of the most powerful and important intuitive gifts is *listening*. It's very underrated and underutilized to the extent that we don't pause to listen to the information from within our hearts first before we stamp it as "truth."

Depending on what kind of a family you were raised in, your inherent natural ability to listen to your heart or listen to others could have been either enthusiastically encouraged or intentionally ignored. The truth is that you can never be unplugged completely from infinite wisdom and from the magic of the Universe, but you can choose to turn your back on your gifts if you forget your power and listen too much to the mainstream narrative of noise.

Here are four methods to help you navigate the modern world of noise:

- Take regular breaks from social media and news feeds. Set limits on your screen time that allow space to recenter yourself.

- Spend quality time in nature, and breathe deeply.

- Keep a journal of your gut instincts and hunches.

- Remember to believe in your own magical powers of intuition.

THE CULTURE OF MAGIC, FOLKLORE, AND SUPERSTITION

In ancient Egypt, magic was part of daily life. In fact, the medical texts of ancient Egypt contain spells as well as what one today would consider practical measures in treating illness, disease, and injury. Another example is how Indigenous cultures all over the world have intuition deeply ingrained and embedded into their lineage and ancestral story lines. The wisdom is passed down from generation to generation to preserve the beautiful knowledge.

It's also extremely important to remember the horrific suppression of knowledge and intuition throughout the ages too—for instance, the countless women over the centuries that were persecuted and accused of witchcraft. Many of them were found guilty and were burned at the stake simply for exhibiting intuitive wisdom or knowledge about how to heal ailments with various types of flora and fauna.

My mother was extremely superstitious when I was growing up. To this day, I will not walk under a ladder. I also held the fear and the belief that if you break a mirror, you'll get seven years of bad luck. Omens and superstitions also have been responsible for some ridiculous reactions and causations to situations in the name of preserving good luck.

For instance, my daughter Ava Moon was born with a tooth. I saw three doctors in Las Vegas that all told me it was a cyst and it was probably nothing to be concerned about. However, I insisted that it was a tooth. It was growing just below the surface of her gums at the bottom of her mouth. I could run my finger over it and feel the tiny ridges. A fourth doctor confirmed my hunch (thank goodness) and stated how rare it was to see a child born with a chomper. Apparently, only one in three thousand children are born with a tooth or a whole set of teeth. In various cultures, this can be perceived as either a lucky omen or a bad one. It can be a sign that the child will become a vampire or a witch, or even that the child must be removed from the community because it brings bad luck and misfortune to a village. And in Malaysian culture, a child born with a tooth is favored because it will welcome in the energy of prosperity. The key distinction here is that our lives should not be dictated by superstition that creates separation with other humans and from our innate intuitive powers of logic. Again, this illustrates that sometimes what is deemed "light and love" is actually limited thinking masquerading as truth.

QUESTION EVERYTHING AND OPEN YOUR HEART TO DISCERNMENT

Intuition helps us in so many ways throughout our lives to discern what's truthful and what's not. For instance, and this is a very lighthearted example, we all have questions we want to know the answers to, and sometimes we seek guidance in the weirdest of ways. I remember I had this Magic 8-Ball when I was about twelve years old. The user asks a yes/no question to the ball and then turns it over to see the answer revealed in a small window on the back of the plastic sphere. I would vigorously shake this novel fortune-telling device to ask if the boy I had a crush on felt the same way.

"Does he like me?" I would ask.

The Magic 8-Ball said no.

I only felt happy and content to put the mystical device down and walk away when it told me what I wanted to hear. I handed my power over to this silly toy and didn't turn to my own powers of discernment for advice, guidance, and wisdom. I used to believe that I had no power or control over what was happening in my life—or in the least how I perceived it to be.

You are in the driver's seat of your own experience. The awareness of this is subtle, but it can make or break your outlook on life. And with obstacles come questions, of course. So when you feel like you have a lot of unanswered questions about your future or why specific things keep happening, it can blur your judgment and make you seek support in the unlikeliest and possibly the most unreliable of places. This often can leave you examining if you are truly on the "right" path and if everything will indeed turn out for the best. When this happens, you need to remember that you are an intuitive person. You probably have all the answers you need within you. It's also important to know that there is no "wrong" path—that everything is an experience that contributes to all the lessons that your soul needs in order to grow.

THE JOURNEY FROM YOUR HEAD TO YOUR HEART

The reality is, although the space between the head and heart is only eighteen inches, most of us spend our entire lives trying to strike a balance between the two. This is because our heads are strong and the thinking center of our human experience. However, the infinite intelligence of the heart center cannot be underestimated. The two work in unison, and for you to spark the magic of intuition, you must be willing to make the journey to understand yourself at the deepest emotional level.

An intuitive person listens to, rather than ignores,

the inner guidance of what their feelings are telling them. One of my favorite words is *clairvoyance*.

Clairvoyance originated from the French words *clair* meaning "clear" and *voyance* meaning "vision," which roughly translates into "one who sees clearly."

Whatever name you prefer to use, whether it's *intuitive*, *medium*, *psychic*, or *clairvoyant* (there are many different modes of connection to the nonphysical realm), the most important piece of integral wisdom to remember is that your inner vision needs to be clear to move forward in life. This is why emotional empowerment and intuition walk side by side throughout life together like the two oxygen atoms that make a molecule.

As humans, we tend to get wrapped up in our thoughts. You've probably heard the saying "Thoughts become things," originating from a man named Prentice Mulford, a well-known humorist and author who lived in Sag Harbor, New York, in the 1800s. It is said that Mulford's musings launched the beginning of the New Thought movement and the beginning of the principles of the law of attraction being released out into the world on a mass scale. I decided to explore this phrase with a new spin on it for the sake of investigating how our intuition contributes to the process of manifestation. I share with my students the concept that "feelings become things." So at this point, you might be asking, "Well, which one is it then, Sarah? Do thoughts become things, or is it feelings?"

It's both. They play together. But emotions are way more powerful to create vibrations (or energy). This is why gratitude can be transformative in times of need. I've practiced this as somewhat of an energy experiment at places that can be hot spots for frustration and energy management—like the Department of Motor Vehicles (DMV) or the post office. At the DMV, my number was at least two hours away from being called, so I had to wait. My phone died, and my focus turned toward the people around me. I decided to send everyone (silently in my mind) the energy of love and appreciation. And soon enough, within less than thirty minutes, my number was called! The remedy to impatience and frustration is definitely to Be the Love. However, first you must discern that it is time to rise above your irritation and create some magic.

In a very simplified explanation, this is how my Be the Love philosophy works: you feel, you heal, and the Universe reveals. First, you tune in to how you intend to feel, then you make peace with what is (which is healing), and then the Universe reveals a path forward. This path usually has signs, dreams, symbols, synchronicities, and steps of inspired action to take. And as long as you embrace your natural intuitive powers (rather than deny them), you will always be guided to the perfect place at the perfect time because you are the oracle.

CREATING YOUR FUTURE VS. PREDICTING IT

From a scientific perspective, everything that exists is moving or oscillating at a specific frequency or vibration. If you place anything under a powerful enough microscope, you can see the atoms all dancing up a storm of movement and potential energy. Simply put, like attracts like, and this is why it's imperative to focus on the feelings that make you feel good and to Be the Love. Your emotions all clump together as vibrations, and the Universe uses them as data points to deliver your reality.

COSMIC CONNECTIONS

It's estimated that over 90 percent of people on this planet believe in a higher power.* Whether you call this power *God* or *Source Energy* or *the Universe*, there is definitely a popular belief that this omnipotent form

---

* Fahmy, Dalia. 2018. "Key findings About Americans' Belief in God." Pew Research Center. April 25, 2018. https://www.pewresearch.org /fact-tank/2018/04/25/key-findings-about-americans-belief-in-god/.

of consciousness resides in all that exists. This is purely my own opinion, but I do believe that the Universe has a plan for us, and that plan is to remember our power to shape our reality with intentional thoughts and feelings. This is the truest way to embody your intuition and levels of discernment.

Life is full of beautiful and mystical mysteries. As an example, lungs look like trees, and trees give us oxygen that helps our lungs to survive. Or how male seahorses are the only male animal in the animal kingdom of living things that can give birth. And then there's the beautiful bridge between science and spirituality—like the Fibonacci sequence or what is known as the golden ratio—a mathematical equation for divine proportions found in nature, used by artists, and in architecture to create harmonious aesthetics. So everything from sacred geometry, rainbows, hummingbirds, shooting stars, and butterflies to the unique nature of a single snowflake—there's no doubt we live in a miraculous Universe of wonder.

However, sometimes we take little detours on the path to becoming better versions of ourselves. Sometimes what we believe is "spiritual" is actually mentalism pretending to be a message from our hearts. It's like someone sneaking into a movie theater to watch the 2:00 p.m. show without paying for a ticket.

Spiritual Bypassing—A Closer Look

There are numerous pitfalls when you are on a spiritual path that can create blind spots, which can be likened to switching lanes in your car without checking your mirrors first. Or, more graphically put, putting rainbow sprinkles on a dog turd and trying to sell it as a delicious treat. This might seem like somewhat of a tough-love observation, but spiritual bypassing is when someone believes they have done all the required work to process their emotions and trauma with new age practices but have yet to endeavor to take all the necessary steps actually required to heal. I know this because I have spiritually bypassed many lessons in life while pretending that I had it all figured out. Clearly, I didn't, which is why I kept returning to the drawing board and was prompted to write this book to walk the talk.

If you ever hear anyone say, "I'm enlightened," then run. Run fast. People that state that they know (without a shadow of doubt) that they understand the secrets of the Universe, or that they can heal you in a single session, are not being truthful. They are practicing spiritual showmanship or showpersonship. Send them love and keep moving. More so, be willing to do the spiritual work required in every step of the journey until the day you die. There are no shortcuts or bypasses. You have to be willing to do the work.

THE AURA READING OF AUTHENTICITY

I am a huge believer in the authentic art of fortune-telling and mediumship. I love crystals, oracle card readings, palmistry, energy healing, astrology, angels, spirit guides, and various other forms of divination. Meeting with a medium is a powerful healing component when a person goes through grieving the loss of a loved one too. It can provide soothing closure even with the tiniest snippets of confirmation and messages from beyond the grave. Ultimately, it's about finding what works for you and trusting the process.

A good psychic will guide you to remember to strengthen and use your own intuitive superpowers. They will reinforce your energy as a sovereign being. The psychics that I have seen over the years have told me various things—like that my sister was going to die in four months, which left me feeling powerless. Or that my son would be born with his bowel *outside* of his body (and that wasn't the case). And by the same token, I have had eerily accurate readings from people that have tuned in on my future with astounding levels of detail.

In 2018, I had an aura reading from a woman in Las Vegas. Vegas is a known hot spot for dodgy readings from shop fronts illuminated with neon lights and credit card payment symbols. They tell you if you'll meet your soul mate soon and what some suggested winning lottery numbers might be. However, I found a unique crystal store that really interested me that didn't show all the telltale signs of being a scam. I opened the door, and there was the tinkle of the wind chimes to notify the shopkeeper that someone was in the store. Celtic flute music was playing, and the shelves were crammed with various spiritual objects, such as candles, crystals, incense, palo santo, boxes of tarot cards, and sage. I felt like I'd stepped into a protected bubble from the surrounding community. It definitely felt like another world, maybe even another time.

"Do I know you?" the lady behind the register said to me. She was wearing a patchwork velvet dress and had giant crystal rings on each finger up to the knuckle on both hands.

My intention was to ask for a reading, and I wanted to do it without the people knowing that I was a manifesting teacher with over a million followers on social media. I'd been recognized in places like this before, so I knew there was a chance that I might not go undetected. If they knew of my work, then I couldn't really relax my energy enough to be read authentically and without bias.

"I must look familiar because I've been in here before," I replied.

I had been in there before for less than thirty seconds with my children—bulls in a china (I mean, crystal) store. Leaving before looking around seemed like the safest and less expensive alternative before the terms of "you broke it, you bought it" were strictly enforced.

"I'm just curious, do you have anyone available to do a reading for me right now?" I asked. I was so interested to see what the Universe would present me with when I made this spontaneous decision. The lady paused for a moment.

"Would you like an aura reading from Bianca? She can be here in just five minutes, if you like."

I'd never had an aura reading before, so this felt exciting, and I agreed. Within less than two minutes, a very petite woman walked in with the energy of intense wisdom. I could feel her presence. She greeted me with a handshake and ushered me to a reading room at the back of the store. The open space before we got to the room looked like it was set up for group gatherings, such as drum circles or collective chanting. I felt slightly uneasy because I'm always so protective when it comes to my energy field. This just basically means that I don't easily allow others into my space. I like to think of my energy field as the gatekeeper to my energy flow and my awareness of what I deem to be sacred.

Bianca then asked me to sit down, and she closed the door.

"We're going to say a prayer together, and then I'm going to take your aura photograph with the Polaroid camera and let's see what's going on." She then started to sage me by lighting on fire a little green bundle of leaves bound together with string and flowers. Apparently, this would cleanse me and open my heart to ancient wisdom.

I felt like I was getting some kind of x-ray or intimate examination from a doctor. I sat in an old-fashioned chair with a white backdrop behind it. It was a portrait setting designed to capture the light. Bianca asked me to open my eyes and told me to hold perfectly still. I heard the click of the camera, and she placed the square image that was birthed out of the device facedown onto the table. She paused and took in a deep and slow breath of consideration. Her eyes then locked with mine, and she was ready to deliver the guidance.

"I'm being told that you need to write a book. You are a messenger. Does that make sense to you?"

Cue the best version of my poker face. I think I tried not to blink to show even the faintest clue that I was a published author.

Bianca flipped over the photo, and there was a vibrant pink-and-purple halo all around my body, especially around my head. I looked at the various photos of her previous clients pinned on the walls, and most of them were either orange, red, or green. I asked why mine was different.

"This is because you have the power to channel wisdom, my dear. You will reach millions upon millions of people. I can really feel this for you."

I couldn't help it—I told her about the book. I told her about my vision and my intention for my upcoming book *Dear Universe*. And then she stopped me in my tracks just as I was about to open my mouth with another sentence.

"No, dear, it's not the book, it's something else. It has nothing to do with the book, actually. I see millions and millions of people watching you from all over the world," she said.

I could feel the truth in what she was saying, and it wasn't just because it was something that felt exciting to hear about. I could feel it in my bones as an experience. There was a grounded humility in this woman that was merging her intuitive gift with mine to do an accurate reading. It felt like an experience in co-creation. It wasn't until over twenty months later that Bianca's prediction made sense with the launch of the Goalcast video and being viewed by over sixty million people. I learned from this glimpse into my future that the vision that Bianca shared with me was not just about the glamourous aspect of the viewing numbers or being so visible, it was the healing journey that would accompany it that would ultimately lead to the creation of this book you are now holding in your hands or listening to.

SHARING INTUITIVE GIFTS
WITH OTHERS

As an intuitive, it's imperative to honor the process, but it's likely that many psychics out there are the fast-food versions of the woo-woo world. I think of sharing my intuition with people as more of a party trick, and I always preface my "readings" with the high possibility of my getting the information wrong. One of the most surreal situations I have found myself in was at a private party in Santa Monica, California, in 2019. As a manifesting and spiritual teacher, I am often mistaken for a medium, which is understandable. People that dabble in the more mystical elements of reality are often seen as holding the answers to life's big questions. If I have your permission or you ask for it, I will share my hunches with you, but not unless you ask and not unless I feel clear enough to deliver empowering information.

There were lots of famous people at this party—authors, CEOs, models, and influencers. Later in the evening, I found myself in a deep conversation with a very well-known Hollywood actor. We connected and felt like kindred spirits at the time, so I offered to walk him through an emotional empowerment exercise that I thought could be helpful for him. I held his hands, and we sat in a state of meditation together for a few minutes before I began walking him through a visualization process to prompt self-forgiveness. There were a few tiny tears rolling down his cheeks with emotion as I spoke. And after a few minutes, I asked him to open his eyes.

"Am I healed?" he asked with a sense of playfulness.

I laughed and said, "Only you can answer that! This is a practice, not a miracle. The more you do this visualization in your own mind, the stronger you will become with your own levels of emotional awareness and intuition. And the best part is that you don't really need me to guide you."

When I was younger, I would have been totally starstruck by this handsome human, unable to interact with him without being like a giddy schoolgirl. But this interaction was different. I felt grounded, and I could see the necessity to remind this man of the power he had to guide his own path to a place of healing and emotional freedom. We all need to turn to the power of creative visualization to make peace with what is.

SIGNS FROM THE UNIVERSE

One of the most powerful ways your intuition speaks to you is through signs and symbols. The purpose of signs is to cultivate a sense of presence and connection and to use it as somewhat of a doorway to your higher self and gut instinct. However, as humans, we love to attach meaning to things to bring a sense of control or certainty. A sign should bring with it a feeling that allows you to activate the magic of the present moment. It doesn't mean if you see a rainbow that you'll win the lottery soon or that there's a pot of gold waiting for you accompanied by a well-behaved leprechaun.

Having said that, though, signs can be delivered in the most incredible ways that leave you feeling blown away with awe and wonder. This reminds me of a powerful experience I manifested when I purchased a simple blue glass water bottle.

One day, I was scrolling through Instagram and noticed an ad for a company that sells water bottles that have sacred spiritual symbols etched into the blue glass. Apparently, these symbols hold an energetic frequency, and you can activate your water with an intention that will ultimately manifest. Now even for me, this seemed a little far-fetched. I visited the online shop and scrolled to the bottle that appealed to me the most. I didn't pay attention to the description of the bottle and what the symbol meant because the words *truth, love, and beauty* were part of the design, and this seemed the best match for what I would like to look at.

I followed the instructions on the little leaflet that was included with my purchase after the bottle arrived. "Fill with clean, filtered water and place in the sun to activate the intention."

"What's that?" Sean asked.

"It's an intention bottle. I know you probably think it's a bunch of nonsense."

I was preparing vegetables to grill out in my garden. I took a sip of my water and then took the tray of bell peppers and sliced zucchini outside to cook. It was a hot summer evening in Las Vegas, and I realized that in my forty years on the planet, I had never cooked on a grill before, so it felt like something I really enjoyed. Then all of a sudden, I heard a hum by the side of my head. It felt as if someone were holding up a tiny fan with a whirring motor. It was a low hum with a breeze. I slowly turned my head to come face-to-face with a hummingbird! I'd seen them in my garden but never up close. This small creature was staring at me, and we held eye contact for over thirty seconds. It had teensy-weensy brown eyes and was looking straight into mine.

It felt like some kind of mystical exchange, almost as if it were an energetic healing of sorts. Later that evening, I, of course, looked up what the spiritual significance of a hummingbird means as a sign. Hummingbirds have a long history of folklore and symbolism in native cultures in the Northern Hemisphere. The Aztecs saw them as messengers from the spirit world between themselves and their ancestors or the gods. In Native American culture, hummingbirds are seen as powerful healers that bring joy, love, and good luck.

And then I remembered the bottle! I went straight to the website and looked up the description for the style of the bottle with my activated intention water that I had only taken one sip out of. It read: "This symbol carries the frequencies of the Hummingbird and the Sacred Divine Feminine."

The symbol included some kind of bird on the bottle—a hummingbird. I couldn't believe it—that something had been activated quite unintentionally and managed to yield such powerful results. I then started carrying this bottle everywhere with me because of the energy I could sense it prompted.

The next morning, Sean and I sat up on my office balcony to watch the sunrise over the Las Vegas mountains. I had my bottle with me, and I was explaining how I was still blown away by what had happened. He still seemed a little skeptical.

"I should get one of those bottles," he said, quite jokingly. And just as he said that, a hummingbird came right up to him in the exact same way it had to me the day before! In the five years we lived in Las Vegas, this had never happened. At the time, we were having a conversation about exploring the possibility of moving from Las Vegas to the Hamptons in New York. It felt like time for our family to explore a new place to live for a while.

"Let's take this as a sign you should go to New York today," I said to Sean. We always loved acting spontaneously to create change, and it made perfect sense for him to go and scout out a possible new home for us to live in.

The flight was leaving in just ninety minutes. He bought a ticket, packed a suitcase, and arrived in Southampton, New York, just seven hours later. Spoiler alert: we did end up moving to the Hamptons for a short time and then returned back to Vegas, which I'll be sharing more about in the next few chapters. Sometimes you just have to go where you are guided for the lessons to reveal themselves.

DO YOU BELIEVE IN COINCIDENCES?

I more strongly believe in these things called *synchronicities*—random events that manifest into your reality that leave you in a pure state of awe due to an intense experience of serendipity. More often than not, you attracted these experiences as a sign of confirmation or as a beautiful wink from the Universe that you are in an excellent state of emotional alignment. I have had synchronicities happen in my own life that have made me question the very nature of reality. Whether it's the humbling reminder that we are all connected, or the soul-stirring awareness that we are so much more than just a physical clump of atoms, it's hard to deny that synchronicities exist for a magical reason.

The first time I experienced a strong synchronicity was when I was in my very last year of high school at Swinburne Senior Secondary College in Melbourne, Australia, in 1997. I was the new girl, and I found myself at a coffee shop near the school in an attempt to make new friends. The previous year had been difficult for me because my mother had sat my sister and me down to reveal that she'd given birth to two babies before I was born. Somewhere out there, I had two half brothers that I knew nothing about, and they probably knew nothing about me. This shook me to my core, because I felt like my whole life had been a lie. Ultimately, my mother withheld the information because she was protecting me in some way. Also it was because she wasn't allowed to contact her sons legally until they were both twenty-one years old. This was the nature of a closed adoption procedure back in New Zealand in the 1970s. In a way, I imagine, she was cautious about exposing my sister and me to the emotional roller coaster of the complex issues relating to the adoption process. If we did reach out to our half brothers, there was a very real chance that they could reject us. Adoption can potentially create a primal wound with numerous complications for all family members involved. Other times, it's simple, natural, and effortless. I have so much love, respect, and admiration for the selflessness and strength my mother had back then and still has. It must have been so incredibly painful to give both of her children to families that could take care of them better than she could at the time.

Within a few months of my mother sharing the news, we met my oldest brother. He was living in New Zealand and looked so much like my mother. He had the exact same curly black hair and gap between his two front teeth. It was disconcerting how much he seamlessly seemed to fit into our family dynamic. The second son also lived in New Zealand but was a bit slower to reconnect. I could imagine it must be daunting to have a birth mother out there that you don't know anything about. We'd seen a photo of this guy and knew his name, but that was it.

So back to the coffee shop at my new school in 1997. I was sitting with these girls who were from New Zealand. An interesting fact is that there are more New Zealanders that live in Australia than live in New Zealand. And there are more sheep in New Zealand than there are New Zealanders. Anyway, even with a small population of just over four million people in Melbourne (the city I grew up in), I thought I would ask this girl, Nicola, if she knew my brother by name—the one that I hadn't met yet.

I went on to tell her the story of the process of being reunited that my parents were currently going through. Nicola looked at me with a strange expression on her face. I mean, out of four million people, why would she know my brother? Because she did! Her ex-boyfriend was his roommate in Wellington, New Zealand! I had so many questions! I wanted to know everything about him, but I had to not be super creepy about it at the same time. What were the odds that in a school of at least eight hundred students, in a city of nearly five million people, that I would meet and make friends with someone who had met my brother, in another country, before I had? The Universe definitely works in mysterious ways, and I'm so glad I followed my hunch to ask Nicola the question.

I've had other synchronicities over the years too that include things like bumping into my husband at Disneyland when we split up for the day to explore the rides. He took our daughter Lulu, and I spent the day with Ava and Olivia. Out of forty thousand daily guests in the five-hundred-acre theme park, I managed to cross paths with my husband at the exact moment we needed to meet up! We had no idea how this happened, considering we hadn't the slightest clue where the other was. It was like finding a needle in a haystack. And then there was a serendipitous experience that will blow our minds forever.

As entrepreneurs that work pretty tirelessly, sometimes we experience emotional burnout. We feel like we've poured so much energy into a launch or supporting our team, and we have days that feel uninspiring and underwhelming.

"Let's go and have a fancy brunch," I said to Sean. I had a splitting headache but thought that getting out of the house would possibly do us a world of good. We lived about a thirty-minute drive from the Las Vegas Strip and loved a place in the Encore casino called Jardin. If you look it up online, it's described as a "garden-inspired space with a patio." They had an amazing vegan breakfast sandwich that was so delicious. Sean and I sat at our table, waited for our sandwiches, and looked a little bit like zombies. I was trying to make conversation but felt like it was somewhat of an effort. This is usually not a problem for Sean and me because we can speak forever and never run out of topics. Today was different, and we were both obviously depleted.

"I'd like to go to Hawaii. You visited when you were a kid, didn't you? What's it like?" I was trying to spark our energy by dreaming of a distant and tropical location we could visit.

"You know what? We should go and visit Joe and Bessy. They said they'd like to catch up if we were ever in Hawaii. I'll text them later." We'd only met Joe and Bessy once, but we'd connected quite deeply at an event I was speaking at in Bali the previous year. They were friends, but new friends. We had exchanged texts and emails only a few times in the last twelve months, so it felt like an inspired idea to reach out and check in again.

On our way home, Sean used an app that would direct us away from any of the congested Las Vegas traffic. Even though the GPS was telling him to go down a certain street, he spontaneously ignored it and made a wrong turn. In Vegas, especially before the pandemic began, the streets were usually crowded with people. The side street that Sean had taken only had one couple, on foot, walking toward the traffic lights to cross the road.

"Oh my gosh, that couple looks a bit like Joe and Bessy!" I said to Sean jokingly because there was no way in the world that could actually be them since we were just talking about them in the restaurant.

"I think that *is* Joe and Bessy! How is this possible? We were only just speaking of them twenty minutes ago!"

We looped the car around the block to make sure it was them, and we still couldn't tell from a distance. Our minds didn't believe it would be possible. Sean decided to text Joe when we got home to confirm if it was indeed them and to share the eerie synchronicity. Apparently, they were in Vegas for only twenty-four hours for a business meeting and our paths just happened to cross. What were the odds? It felt like the Universe was amplifying our energy and attracting to us the people and places we were speaking about. I'll be talking more about speaking things into reality in chapter 6, "Your Word Is Your Wand."

THE MEANING

When things like this happen and blow your socks off, it's important to remember not to look too deeply for an inherent meaning behind it. I see events like this as a reminder that we are part of a much bigger picture at play.

One creative idea is to keep an intuition journal or notebook with you to record your hunches, your dreams, or your feelings. Just like working out a muscle in a gym, you must build your strength intuitively for it to truly serve you.

Collective Kindness Exercise 2

Share a piece of music or art with a friend. Sharing creative energy and the appreciation of artistry activates intuitive energy in your heart. Alternatively, share one of your most recent vivid dreams with someone.

THINGS THAT HELPED ME TO ACTIVATE MY INTUITION:

1. **I learned how to trust my gut and to remember that vibes don't lie:** I used to make quick decisions that were purely based on what my gut was telling me. This left a lot of room to make mistakes or foolish judgments without understanding the full landscape of a situation before either jumping in with a yes or backing out with a hard no. Now I learn to gather all the pieces of information when making a decision, and I do a gut check within my heart to make sure that I'm aware of all my blind spots before making a move. However, sometimes there are split-second moments of intuitive action that are really important to follow when my heart feels guided.

2. **I kept a dream journal to record my nightly dreams:** It's really easy to forget what your dreams are when you wake up in the morning. Something that I found really effective and fascinating is to keep a dream journal beside my bed just in case I had something interesting visiting me in the dream world.

3. **I learned to guide my energy, trust my gut, and question narratives:** In my midtwenties, I would receive phrases that I knew were important to practice. By *receive*, I mean that it came to me in some form of a

download of words. The two phrases were *Rise above it* and *Spend your energy wisely.* These two phrases are powerful to guide your energy when you might be handing it over to external influences.

4. **I surrounded myself with sacred reminders of my intuitive powers:** Whether it's jewelry that holds a specific meaning, frequency, or intention; or crystals, candles, or special glass water bottles, I felt more guided to remember my powers when I set up a sacred space in my home for my spiritual goodies. These soulful trinkets help to support my energy and ground my awareness back into the present moment. I am a big believer in the energy of mystic mentors, so I have statues or pieces of jewelry that represent ascended masters, such as Guanyin, the Buddhist goddess of compassion, or the Hindi goddess of prosperity, Lakshmi.

5. **I learned how to create spaciousness for answers to come to me:** Over the years, whenever I would have a panic attack, it felt like the walls were closing in around me. I couldn't breathe, and my heart would feel as though it were going to jump right out of my chest. I learned how to create spaciousness within meditation. As soon as you close your eyes and breathe deeply, you release even the tiniest fragments of resistance and find your safe space. The more I practiced meditation, the more I felt extremely spacious within and

clearer answers would come to me. And it was from this state of spaciousness that I experienced feelings of openness, of trust, and of surrender. This was particularly helpful when I was feeling like I needed answers because I could intentionally guide my experience by turning inward, rather than outward for comfort.

JOURNAL PROMPTS: Be the Love and Remember That You Are the Oracle

FEEL: What are specific ways that your body communicates insight and wisdom to you and through you? Do you feel it in your heart, your gut, or your bones? What excites you the most about embracing your natural gifts of intuition?

_____

_____

_____

_____

HEAL: How can you begin to nurture a better relationship with your intuition? What are some ways that you have been accurate with your hunches and gut instincts over the years?

_____

_____

_____

_____

REVEAL: What are signs and symbols that you would feel are messages directly for you from your higher self and the Universe? Have you ever manifested something that you knew was going to happen?

_____

_____

_____

_____

3

Outside Your Comfort Zone

Close your eyes, breathe in deeply, exhale, and then say this affirmation: *I am ready.*

It feels safe to be comfortable. Everyone has a comfort zone. Once boundary lines are crossed, feelings of fear can activate. It's the unpleasant feelings of eating food that is too hot, running until your legs hurt, waking up too early, or plunging into icy-cold water. The space outside your comfort zone is supposedly where the magic happens. And it's so true that the greatest amount of growth happens in direct proportion to the amount of discomfort you experience along the way. The trouble is that most people don't feel ready for change, because change is scary. It's the ultimate fear of the unknown. This is why I love the saying that there are many blessings that reveal themselves in the lessons. Or another way of putting it: "No pain, no gain." I resonate with this saying because I have ridden the wave of fear probably more times than a record-breaking surfer. I've crashed, wiped out, been nearly drowned by the waves, and then picked myself back up consistently more times than I care to count. Each time, I'm a little bit stronger and somewhat better prepared. As an example, I felt so afraid to open my heart up to love again after my first marriage ended. I felt extremely scared that I would never be able to support my children financially and keep a roof over their heads. There have also been times when I was extremely nervous that my business would fail. Every step of the journey, I didn't feel ready for change. Even entertaining fearful thoughts of worst-case scenarios that prompt change is something I still struggle with to this very day. I worry about earthquakes, choking, being stung by killer bees, slipping on a wet bathroom floor, and the infinite amount of anxiety-ridden ways that one of my loved ones could potentially be harmed. But the choice I have in each and every moment is to view each hurdle with a willingness to be brave and to get comfortable with uncertainty. This is usually how I talk myself down from the ledge of my own limitations because ultimately, fear attracts fear.

One of my greatest fears was being afraid of my own potential to live life on my own terms. To do this, just like I have mapped out for you here in this book, required deep levels of bravery, raw honesty, and facing painful pieces of truth within my heart. For healing to take place, I knew that I had to venture out of my comfort zone into unexplored realms of emotional responsibility. Simply put, I had to own my shit and not make others responsible for my happiness.

I am driven by integrity to let you know that I've had verbal permission from my ex-husband to share what unfolded in our marriage over the years. We've had healing conversations, and even though some of the actions and words are hurtful, we both know that we are not those people anymore. We grew, we changed, and we offered one another forgiveness—which is one of the greatest gifts we could offer our children. After all the violence we shared, holding on to grudges for one another for years seemed like a waste of life force energy. With that being said, let's track back a little to how our emotional pain would manifest.

MEAN AND NASTY

In 2009, my ex-husband pulled out every dirty trick in the book. I also believe that he knew that I was terrified of being alone because I never had been up until that point. This is how he meticulously tended to plant the seeds of fear and doubt into my mind. Or at least, I was under the impression that he had that power over me to do so. I don't even believe this was a conscious process for him, because underneath all the pain and suffering was a man with a beautiful heart that I fell in love with in 1999. Even if I did one day build up the courage to leave him, he knew I wouldn't be brave enough to follow through, or even have the heart to stay away for very long because I loved him so much. Our love was as toxic as adding a cupful of nail polish to a green smoothie.

"You'll never survive as a single mother out there, Sarah. Plus, no one will love you with a spare tire around your middle like that." He had said way worse things than this over the years, and so had I. Our mutual pain was like a twin tornado sweeping through every last saving grace of our relationship.

I would tell him he was like a robot and incapable of connection with other human beings on an authentic level. I would tell him he was useless, neglectful, selfish, and unintelligent. As a corporate wife back then, I am ashamed to say that in social situations, I would be quite mean and demeaning because I knew that he wouldn't get violent with me in front of other people—especially his peers.

I usually felt scared that if I pushed the limits too far, his anger could spiral even more out of control—as could mine. I would belittle him in front of important business colleagues in an attempt to create comic relief at his expense. I would say things like my head could literally be on fire and he wouldn't notice because he would get so fixated and focused on other things. My jokes tended to go over his head anyway usually (and also would go unnoticed), so I assumed that he didn't care. This was one of the ways that my levels of resentment were manifesting over time. I completely forgot to honor his need as a human being to feel loved and seen as well. I remember that the deafening silence during a car ride home was one of the key indicators of an impending explosion—the calm before a storm. It could have been that I'd said something mean. It could have been that my skirt was too short and I looked like a slut. Or it could have been that I was talking to a man for too long and conversing could translate as flirting. I rarely knew the triggers but could bet my bottom dollar that it was something I did or said to set him off.

During the beginning of our relationship, I didn't speak up for my needs for the first two years. I had no idea how to use my voice and share my opinion. I think he liked it this way initially since I was quite a naive nineteen-year-old girl when we met, and he was thirty-one. However, as my levels of empowerment and maturity were growing over the years, he became even more withdrawn and more intense with his opinions of who he thought I should be and what I was capable of becoming. In a conversation we had many years later in 2020, he shared with me that we are only capable of what we *believe* we are capable of achieving. This shows me the immense personal growth and emotional healing he has experienced over the last thirteen plus or so years since we divorced.

When I was nine months' pregnant with my second child back in 2005, he would go out drinking all night with his work buddies and forget to take his house keys with him. He did this at least twice. At 4:00 a.m., there would be a knock at the door after the taxi would drop him off. I'd intentionally take my time to get to the door and then point him toward the couch for him to sleep on, because the stench of alcohol was so overbearing.

I'm not proud of it, but one night, I was having mild contractions, and because I was unable to drive, I relied on him to be able to take me to the hospital if the baby decided to arrive early. I went to the laundry room, filled up a bucket of ice-cold water, and poured it over him while he was deeply sleeping in his drunken state! Shamefully, as a grown woman, no matter how vengeful, underestimated, or hurt I felt, it still didn't give me an excuse to behave in this way. When my words didn't work, I turned to actions. And sometimes my own violent actions were fueled by rage.

I believe we were trying to keep each other small. His verbal abuse would make me question myself at every turn. We got seriously nasty at the end of our marriage and were attacking one another for how we express ourselves sexually. It was underhanded and spiteful. The energy held the intention to break us. And it worked, because I truly believed that I was broken and would never amount to much if I was all on my own out in the world. I had quit college twice with two-thirds of a degree in psychology and journalism. I hadn't been to a regular job in nearly nine years. My husband was the breadwinner, and because child care cost so much money in Australia, it didn't make sense for me to work just to be away from the kids all day. He was always dreaming of the day when both children would be at school so I could go and get a job in a coffee shop to finally contribute to the household. This was a fair request, but I never felt like he acknowledged the hard work I did in our household, such as cooking, cleaning, laundry, shopping, and raising our two children while he was at work for fifty hours a week and returned home to a hot meal and clean, folded underwear. In my heart of hearts, I always felt like I had bigger plans because my entrepreneurial spirit was consistently calling for me to step into the greatest version of myself.

In truth, I was so scared of being on my own even though I had felt so lonely and isolated for most of the time we were married. I was scared of breaking free, I was scared of leaving my marriage, I was scared of being alone with myself. In fact, being alone was the most terrifying aspect of the whole ordeal. The bottom line was that I was afraid to change, because any change that I tried to manifest was met with intense resistance within my heart.

STOLEN MOMENTS

I started flourishing emotionally in the stolen moments when the children were either asleep, at school, or occupied with their toys. I had a laptop and an internet connection, and I was committed to learning everything I could about creating an online business. I would tirelessly search the internet for articles on how to start blogging, how to use social media, and how to create an ebook to sell online. I felt intuitively that creating an online business based on my love for teaching spiritual concepts was the key to my freedom. The very first ebook I wrote was called *You and the Universe,* which was a basic introductory course to using the law of attraction. I saw that other people were selling their ebooks on eBay (this is not allowed anymore, by the way), and I knew that if I created a fancy cover, I could potentially get some sales, which I did, and I became instantly hooked. Along the way, I started using Twitter. This was in the days before it was picked up by mainstream media and utilized by news outlets. This was where my passion for teaching spirituality really started to blossom. I would write funny statements, ask questions, share my ebook, connect with others, offer advice, and see a community starting to build and flourish around me. I felt safe, understood, and seen. I started to feel a little less lonely too, which was nice.

Now that I was earning a little money from my eBay adventures and growing quite a large following (around ten thousand followers on Twitter), I was invited to attend a networking event. Actually, it was called a tweetup instead of a meetup. I asked my husband to "babysit" for the evening so I could go and meet the strangers on the internet I had been connecting with.

I walked into the bar. It was somewhat smoky and crowded with unfamiliar faces. In the corner was a guy I had shared a few tweets with named Howard. He had green eyes the color of aventurine and seemed friendly. He waved me over to sit next to him, and we felt instantly connected. There was a vague hint of familiarity that I was intrigued by. Since we clicked and hit it off, he asked me if I wanted to meet up for a coffee or go out for lunch sometime. I didn't think it would be a date, because I had a wedding ring on my finger and had mentioned my husband several times during our conversation. And since I had just met the guy, I wasn't going to spill my guts about how bad my marriage was. All I knew is that I liked this guy and it felt really natural to want to spend more time with him, so I did.

For the first time in my adult life, I felt like I was being truly seen by someone. In reality, it was because I was starved of flowing conversation, natural chemistry, and masculine attention due to different levels of shame manifesting in every intricate corner of my marriage.

THE CATALYST AND THE COWARD

My husband took the afternoon off work to look after the children so I could go door-to-door visiting various bookstores to see if they would be willing to stock my self-published book. Since my ebook did so well, I gave self-publishing a try.

"Hey there, darling, just checking in. I've already had three bookstores show interest—which is great. I want to stay out a few more hours to see if I can get some more whole-sale orders. Is that okay with you?" I lied, and I sounded convincing. There was a tremor of excitement in my voice from the nervousness of not telling the truth.

An hour later, I was feeling smooth sheets against my bare skin in Howard's bed. I went there. I breached every code of my moral compass, and I found myself having sex with a man who was not my husband. It felt great at the time—I was fully present, grounded in my body, witnessing the powerful impact of newness. And then when I returned home, the dark shadow of shame hung over my head like a cloud that wouldn't go away.

Everywhere I went, there was the shame, and it didn't leave me until many years later. I felt like a coward.

THE CONFESSION

The day I confessed my wrongdoings to my husband is a day I will never forget. We were in our bedroom, and he knew something was wrong. I could see it on his face. He was sitting on our bed, and I was leaning up against the wall by the dresser.

"What's the matter? You know you can tell me anything, right?" He sounded sympathetic, but it felt like a trap. He rolled his eyes and sighed. "Did you scratch the car again?"

I shook my head.

"Did you overspend your budget again this month?"

I shook my head.

"You didn't sleep with someone else, did you?" He said it jokingly, but there was a hint of curiosity and knowing. We might not have been tremendously emotionally connected, but his intuition was quite often on point. The tears were flowing down my face like they were being squeezed from my shame cloud. It was time to confess.

"I did sleep with someone else, but it was only once, and I really, really regret it. I'm so sorry. I don't know what to say. It was a guy I met at the Twitter meetup, and I think I have feelings for him."

My husband paused and was thoughtful with his response to instantly go into solution mode.

"Here's what you're going to do. I want you to go and break it off with this guy, and we'll work this out. Take some time for yourself today to clear your head."

I left the house that afternoon, and as the Goalcast video explains in painstaking detail, I returned that evening to a war zone. In my absence, my husband had destroyed all my belongings in a drunken rampage. Glasses were smashed, precious letters were ripped, my clothes were all ruined. And the worst part was that he was looking after the children, who heard everything and were terrified. There were piles of puke in different locations throughout the house, and my laptop was smashed with a hammer. It was a jealous rage, and it was a blessing that it was not directed at me in the form of physical violence.

It was 3:00 a.m., and I called my dad in the middle of the night because I didn't know what to do. He told me to call the police, and that's the first time I had ever asked for outside assistance and support. My dad lived not very far away and was on my doorstep within ten minutes to see the extent of the destruction. After the two police officers arrived, I felt so emotionally strong right up until I had to state the names and birth dates of my children. The other officer cuffed my husband and escorted him out to the car. I noticed he was barefoot, and so I was rushing around the house to try to find him a pair of socks so that his feet didn't get cold. This was a classic people-pleasing move. Even in this state of extreme emotional chaos, I was still trying to gain approval and do the right thing.

He spent that night in a jail cell. And after his court appearance on Monday morning, we had an intervention order in place from the court that had a long list of legal boundaries that he was not allowed to cross or I would call the police and get him arrested again. The list included verbal abuse, physical abuse, financial control, and various other forms of threatening behavior. The judge was extremely reluctant to grant us an intervention order while we were living under the same roof, but I was still protecting all his levels of comfort and making excuses for him at every turn. The police officer wanted to press official charges, and I refused to let it go that far.

Meanwhile, the violent actions of my husband had made me feel closer to Howard, my new lover. I turned to him emotionally to help me get through this extremely difficult emotional time. Howard was a rescuer, and I needed and wanted to be rescued. It was my pattern for dealing with pain.

SHINE LIKE THE SUN

Let's just say that Howard was an interesting character. With an intellect that was off the charts, he could have been one of the smartest people I have ever met in my life to this very day. He offered me great perspective and wisdom with incredible levels of self-awareness. In the beginning, I didn't understand how someone so amazing would choose to be with someone as broken as I was. Howard was also a shaman of sorts—an energy healer. He could reach into your energy field and pull out monstrous, octopus-shaped obstructions from your aura. I definitely believed I had more than a calamari salad hindering my field of energy. Truthfully, I never really understood what this healing modality was all about because, even for me, this seemed a little far-fetched.

Within just eight weeks of meeting Howard, I had moved in with him. He moved out of his bachelor pad, which overlooked the bright city lights of Melbourne, to live in the suburbs with me and my two children in a house that we rented and could afford. The two-story house had a white picket fence, which made it seem warm and inviting—a great place for a fresh start. Over the back fence was the headquarters of the Hells Angels chapter of Melbourne—a motorcycle club that was often occupying news headlines because they would get into trouble with the police. Let's just say Friday and Saturday evenings were lively and unpredictable.

My new relationship moved almost too fast. I remember meeting with the Realtor to sign the lease papers, and they addressed the children and assumed that Howard was their father. I witnessed the looks on their faces as they didn't bother to correct the assumption. When you know that your kids are in emotional pain, you do everything you can to reassure them. I positioned this move as an adventure and that we would be safe. I promised them that Mummy would be happy with Howard and this was the beginning of our new life—a selfish move, for sure.

I didn't have any money, and Howard's income was extremely limited as a software coder. Together, we had grand dreams of creating a thriving online enterprise. The intention was that we would support each other in our independent business projects, and of course we were off to a flying start with my loyal Twitter following. At times, we would visualize the life we wanted to create in the evening before going to sleep. We would imagine a large home, happy children, and boundless abundance.

My daughter was just three at the time, and she was having meltdowns of epic proportions. It seemed like even the smallest of things was triggering her and the emotions of the situation were too big for her tiny body to contain. This, sadly, was very reminiscent of my own childhood issues. Howard didn't know how to manage her, and I sure didn't. Her outbursts were pure, untamed rage. I knew she was processing her emotional pain, but I didn't know how I could best help her and offer her support. My son, on the other hand, was eight, and he kept his feelings very contained and private. I could tell that in many ways, he felt a reprieve from the burden of many years of violence in the house. I could see him relaxing and healing for one of the first times ever. Thomas and Olivia are extremely resilient and resourceful humans. I am so proud of the people that they have become despite having to keep up with all my mistakes.

When we first lived with Howard, the day-to-day routine of keeping a clean house, washing laundry, cooking meals, and dropping Thomas off at school felt incredibly natural. There were moments I would catch myself wondering if I was on the right path or if I had made a terrible mistake. On one hand, having sex with a man that wasn't my husband felt exciting. For the first time in a long time, I felt like I could explore my likes and dislikes in the bedroom. Howard knew his way around my body and would help me with my mind-set to embrace all my perceived flaws. He told me my wrinkly stomach was beautiful. He told me my stretch marks were incredible. I felt seen.

When you're living with someone, you really get

to know them on a whole new level. Within about two weeks, I started seeing that my problems had been transplanted into a different location. We'd invite friends over and pretend that we were beginning this union with a clean slate, but we both knew that wasn't the case. There were giant elephants in the room that were leaving many of the biggest questions unanswered. I was still very much in battle mode and ready for a fight at any given moment. Howard, on the other hand, was a peace-loving person who wasn't tolerating my emotional violence. There was only so much time that I was willing to play house before the layers of trauma needed to be revealed.

Howard and I were friends with this other guy on Twitter. He worked in the personal development industry and lived in Hollywood. In fact, my friendship with this guy felt so natural and genuine because he was helping me to navigate my feelings during this time of great emotional upheaval. We met on Twitter and then moved to email as great friends. He would often tweet something to me, and Howard would mention our obvious connection.

"You know, if you and I don't work out, I can totally see you ending up with Sean Patrick Simpson."

I dismissed this comment immediately. First, Sean lived on the other side of the world. Second, he was five years younger than I was. And third, I had just started my brand-new life with Howard, and he was willing to make such a bold statement in saying that I could potentially thrive with another man. It was risky, and I had no idea how deeply intuitive and profoundly prophetic this statement would turn out to be. I wonder if he knew that I would end up marrying Sean just four years later? I remember Howard referring back to this statement, saying that he had the worst superpowers ever to be able to predict who his girlfriend would end up with next.

Living with Howard was magical at first. Life felt like an exciting adventure. However, I distinctly remember that my mother told me that you cannot leave one man for another. And oh boy, was she right!

My mother lived in another state at this stage and decided to fly down for Thomas's ninth birthday and kill two birds with one stone. She would meet my new man, see my new place, and assess how stable I was emotionally (or so I assumed). Howard had nice furniture, and our combined book collection made us look like a very complementary couple—it was spirituality meets personal development. I desperately wanted my mother's official tick of approval even if it was superficial. I just needed someone to tell me that the way my shame was manifesting made sense and was completely understandable. On a subconscious level, I think I knew that I was punishing myself for having an affair by living with Howard and trying to seek safety with another man.

At the end of my mother's stay, I distinctly remember a conversation we had at the airport as she was about to fly back home to the Sunshine Coast. I knew that she was intentionally trying to pick the right moment to say, "You know, you don't have to stay with him, Sarah. You could come up to Queensland and be with me for a while, if you'd like."

Those words opened a portal for me. If anything, they gave me permission to do something for myself. I loved Howard, but I was in no position to rush straight out of my marriage to be with him. I needed to be a single mother for a while and get to know myself as an adult woman. I had never done that before, and in a way, I felt so selfish for being so paralyzed by fear of the unknown and my reluctance to venture out of my comfort zone. But entertaining the option to truly be single felt exciting. Who would I be if I was on my own? What would it feel like not to have to consider anyone else? Would removing the safety net of needing a man help to empower my children? Would it help them to heal? Would it help me to heal?

Howard was sad, but ultimately he understood that our love story was a case of really bad timing. On the day I moved all my things out of our house, he left a book as a parting gift. It was called *The Vortex* by Esther Hicks, all about the law of attraction. On the inside cover, he inscribed a message: *Shine like the sun, Sarah Prout.*

And that's exactly what I decided to do next.

THE WORK BEGINS AND NEVER ENDS

I had to forgive myself for having the affair, for being a mess, for dragging my children along for the journey, for being violent, and for tolerating abuse, and it was so, so hard. I'm not going to sugarcoat it here, but what I will say is that time does heal a lot of wounds.

It was July 31, 2018, and I decided to join my ex-husband and our kids for dinner the night he arrived in Las Vegas from Australia. It had been three years since we had all been together and since I'd moved to the United States. Thomas and Olivia felt extremely nervous to have their parents in the same space and to visit with their father.

Most people would close the chapter of a failed marriage behind them if they managed to escape our level of violence. Most people would leave and never look back. Despite our painful history, I chose to get curious and explore the present moment with my ex-husband. I was interested in understanding who he had become and how he had healed. I also wanted him to see who I had become too. I was no longer a timid, voiceless, subservient girl running around trying to find socks. I was the exact version of the person I'd fought so hard to become.

Did he realize the strength it required to build my life from nothing? Did he understand that there were days when I was hungry because I couldn't afford food? Was he aware that my heart had to repair itself from soul-shattering trauma to truly connect with my new husband? Does he understand that I have forgiven him, and I honor him for our experience together?

The questions left unsaid had an urgency behind them. For the first time in many years, we sat together eating dinner. It was a little weird at first. I sat across from him, and we chatted about life and boring details. I asked about his brother, his new wife, and his parents. Then I told him that I wrote a book called *Dear Universe*, which wouldn't have been possible without him and our volatile marriage. I did it: I went there.

"Names have been changed to protect the innocent, I hope!" he said jokingly.

I explained to him that *Dear Universe* was born and written from my loneliness and my desire to take responsibility for my own happiness and to heal my emotional pain—that a tiny, lonely moment on New Year's Eve in 2008 was the very beginning of my path of empowerment.

"Congratulations," he said with such a genuine tone.

I never would have thought in a million years that

I would be sitting peacefully at a dinner table with my ex-husband, exchanging pleasantries. The energy that fueled our mutual violence for so many years had vanished like dissolving a spoonful of sugar in a hot cup of tea.

I had forgiven him. I had forgiven myself. The blessing was also the opportunity to express to him that there was a divine purpose to the pain—that beyond just creating two beautiful children together, the Universe had actually worked through us to inspire millions of people. I expressed the deep honor of the pain—ultimately the divine plan.

More often than not, we can't see the lesson and the purpose when we're in the midst of the emotional distress. We tend to always get so wrapped up in the wrongness. We're blinded by blame, entitlement, and judgment.

The famous Sufi poet Rumi once wrote:

Out beyond ideas of wrongdoing and rightdoing, there is a field. I'll meet you there.

At this moment with my ex-husband, in the restaurant in Las Vegas, I was sitting in that field beyond fear. I was no longer carrying the label of *adulteress,* and he was no longer a *wife beater.* We were just two people in the surrendered state of forgiveness. Don't get me wrong—it was still super awkward! However, there was a full-circle layer of completion that was in the process of being initiated.

I had butterflies of newness in my stomach—it was a weird sensation. It was like the release of a full spectrum of physical heaviness that I had carried for so many years. My body and my heart had been my steadfast companions every step of the journey, sending powerful feedback that I had ignored.

This is why it's imperative to tune in to the ways your body speaks to you and the lessons that are readily available to discern if you're brave enough to explore. Your body is providing constant feedback to let you know if you are on the right path or not.

THE PHYSICAL MANIFESTATION OF FEAR

Bali, Indonesia, 2019

I couldn't swallow, and my throat was closing up like a clamshell. It felt like a strep infection burning up my tonsils and couldn't have arrived at a worse time. I was scheduled to be onstage in the next twelve hours, and this was my first big keynote speech. It was a huge deal for me. Sean and I were staying in the most beautiful resort in Bali, Indonesia. I was initially scared to say yes to this opportunity because I have always held a fear that I would die in a tsunami; I'd had a recurring nightmare for over the last thirty-plus years that the sky would be filled with a wall of water headed toward the land, and then I suddenly wake up at the exact moment that my lungs fill with liquid. Yes, this is a tad dramatic. However, Indonesia, a country made up of more than seventeen thousand islands, is part of the infamous and super-scary Ring of Fire. This ring of fire felt like it was manifesting in the back of my throat on the day of my first keynote speech. These tsunami dreams often come to me in times of emotional upheaval, which happens from time to time. So before I said yes to the speaking gig, I studied the hotel for their tsunami emergency evacuation routes. Fearful and expecting the worst? I was indeed.

I'd been living in the United States for three years, and so it felt strange to be so close to Australia without visiting home, but the tropical paradise was unlike anything I had ever experienced before. The temples held quiet wisdom that complemented the exquisite flora and fauna. My hair extensions were taped in, feeling very itchy, and they didn't like the Balinese heat and humidity. I had to make peace with not having perfect hair onstage, and that was okay. What I didn't anticipate was that this throat issue would weaken my voice. Sean gently and compassionately asked if I could be potentially sabotaging myself. He felt that my throat chakra needed to be cleared and that if I rested, I would be okay enough to complete the gig. Sean is tremendously intuitive and knows when to offer support in my times of need.

I'd been through two rounds of speaker training to become confident in delivering a great keynote. This newfound tool of using my voice felt powerful and unknown, like having a fast car and not wanting to step on the gas to see how fast it could run. And yet, I was still terrified. *What if the giant wave crashes through the conference when I am onstage? What if I cry? What if I forget my words? What if my heels are too high and I land on my face?*

When I get nervous, so do my bowels. My mind runs through all the possible worst-case scenarios. I couldn't relax until this keynote was delivered, done, and dusted. After the glam team was finished with me in my suite, I headed over from my room to the backstage area to get hooked up to a microphone for the sound check. I knew that if I could deliver this speech from my heart, then I would do a good job. I also knew that the upcoming gigs would be way better with practice.

I waited in the wings as the incredibly talented emcee introduced me, and then I was center stage, delivering my keynote speech. It felt different from how I ever could have anticipated. There was an energetic connection between the audience and me. It was a flow of intention and feedback. I would speak, and they would respond. I could only see the faces of the people in the front row, but what I could see was a unified reaction and reception. After I finished, the crowd applauded, and I walked off the stage. I had done it! My throat was fine, and I had my very first official speaking gig under my belt. I allowed myself to be visible, and I didn't realize how amazingly freeing it would feel. This was definitely a rewarding full-circle moment when I had been brave enough to venture out of my comfort zone. Remember, I was a timid child with extreme anxiety issues, and this was one of the first times in my life that I'd felt empowered to stand up and use my voice without fear of not being accepted.

That night, all the attendees of the event dressed up as fairies and mythical creatures to board buses to be taken to a secret party location. My forehead was covered in stick-on rhinestones, and I had to fold and carry my wings on my lap during the mystery trip. The bus drove down narrow Balinese streets, and the humid air was warm and comforting. Upon arrival, we were at a park on a cliff overlooking the ocean. We walked down a corridor of fairy lights to the most magical party of elves, wizards, pixies, and fairies. The most incredible deejay was on the stage blasting the best dance music, the alcohol was flowing freely, and I had the pure essence of relaxation flood my entire body after delivering my keynote without a hitch. And then, when we least expected it, the heavens opened. It poured with rain.

It poured with rain, and the music kept playing. What happened next was fascinating. People started to flock undercover because they didn't want to get wet. The people who didn't care seized the moment and danced up a storm! The people who were reluctant huddled together like chickens in a henhouse on a chilly evening.

I made the conscious choice to be one of those people to seize the moment and not be afraid of the water. We danced for hours in the warm rain, in puddles that then turned to mud, and with the full awareness that this evening would be magical and memorable.

Remember my analogy in chapter 1 where I referred to those derelict houses perched on a cliff about to fall into the sea as my fragile sense of self-worth? I drew the parallel where I felt like the connection with myself was about to fall into the ocean. Well, on this beauteous night, I was fully myself—the full manifestation of Sarah Prout—dressed in a fairy costume with wings and wearing a crown. Even dancing in public was a turning point from fear for me, and I loved it. I also loved that there was no tsunami.

STRENGTH, COURAGE, AND WISDOM

You are so much stronger than you think you are. Of course there are many things that can happen in life that can impact how confident and capable you feel in any given situation. The key thing to always hold close to your heart is that you are a resilient soul. So if (and when) life knocks you down and presents you with opportunities to grow, you must remember to get back up again. Don't see defeat, frustration, or perceived failure as an excuse to tap yourself out of the game and sit on the sidelines. You are so strong and capable. This is what I have told myself each and every time I face a hurdle in my life.

The fear you may experience in moments where you are fully immersed in the mirage of uncertainty often presents you with a choice of how you will respond to it. In that moment, you can ask yourself several powerful questions that prompt inner reflection.

- How can I send my fearful thoughts love?
- What is the worst thing that can happen if my fears come true?
- How can I be more loving and compassionate to myself in moments of fear?
- How can I embody the energy of love?
- How can I completely accept my current reality right now?

And most importantly, how can I Be the Love?

Be willing to challenge yourself a little bit on a daily basis. It's often said that growth happens when you do something uncomfortable or that you thought would be too complicated at least once a day. I'm not saying that you should place yourself in dangerous situations daily that make you feel scared, like putting a scorpion in your mouth or walking on hot coals. I'm saying that it's so beneficial to examine the boundaries of your goals and see how you can exceed your own perceived limits. You could run an extra mile, or spend ten more minutes on your yoga mat, or drink two extra glasses of water in a day. The point here is to expand your mindset and create a collection of experiences where you can prove to yourself that you are indeed capable of venturing out of your comfort zone.

Collective Kindness Exercise 3

Next time you hear someone achieve something amazing, make it your priority to congratulate them for their willingness to try something new. This will make someone's day when you acknowledge them for venturing out of their comfort zone. Supporting the success of others contributes to the collective energy of celebration.

THINGS THAT HELPED ME TO VENTURE OUT OF MY COMFORT ZONE

1. **I lowered the stakes:** Do you ever build things up in your mind too much and make them more of a big deal than they actually are? When this happens, you're more than likely to talk yourself out of whatever you might be considering doing. When the time came to make decisions or act, I would hold the belief that the outcome would have a catastrophic impact on my life in some way and that the stakes were too high to even try. When I started becoming aware of my defeatist pattern, I would ask myself questions like, *Well, Sarah, what's the worst thing that could happen if you didn't do X?* The more I started to not be so intense with my approach toward the outcome of things, the more I let go of control, and things usually still worked out for the best.

2. **I embraced failure:** When I first started to learn how to speak onstage, I felt as timid as a mouse. My voice was quiet, my shoulders were rounded, and my core felt weak. I was at a three-day speakers' boot camp and knew that the speech I had prepared for assessment was seriously going to suck. However, I knew that even if I failed that the next speech would be better and give me experience to build upon. My speech did suck. I cried, and I was very spilly with my

emotions to the point that it diluted the intention of the speech. At that point, I embraced failure because I viewed each misstep as a bridge to improvement. When you fail, get back up again and keep going. The Universe will always reward your willingness.

3. **I took a leap of faith:** You can either stay stuck or you can dance your way out of your comfort zone into the sweet space of success. I was terrified to stand on a stage in front of possibly thousands of people and deliver a keynote speech. My mentor reminded me that if I'm prepared, I shouldn't be scared. Learning the skill of speaking in front of others was way out of my comfort zone, but I committed to doing it because I knew that it would help me to reach and impact more people around the world. Ask yourself how you can say yes to additional scary and exciting opportunities in your life. It's the gateway to your growth as a human being.

4. **I stopped using fear as an excuse:** For many years, when Sean and I first started the business, I refused to be on camera and do video, much to his frustration. I refused because I was afraid of how I would be perceived, and I was too self-conscious to feel comfortable delivering a message. He wondered how on earth we could scale our business if I didn't want to be seen. Whenever you feel fear in the pit of your stomach, ask yourself how you could possibly venture

out of your comfort zone to where the magic happens.

5. **I accessed the magic of the present moment:** Have you heard the saying that there's no time like the present? Well, it's true. There are three things that help you snap into the present moment faster than a flash of lightning: cold water, deep meditation, or sex. All three are fabulous ways to meet the moment with a sense of awe and wonder. It gets you out of your head and into your heart every single time. If you feel afraid or trapped in your emotions in some way, then grounding yourself in your body is the perfect approach to feeling more empowered to take inspired action.

JOURNAL PROMPTS: Be the Love and Venture Out of Your Comfort Zone

FEEL: What are you most afraid of in life? What is the worst thing that could happen to you? What is the best thing that could happen to you? What are you most excited about that could happen as a result of venturing outside of your comfort zone?

HEAL: What specific and defining experiences have you had in life that either made you afraid of change or made you embrace it? What signs, cues, or hunches would manifest for you to either let you know you were in alignment, or give you a fully grounded YES response in your body?

REVEAL: What are three steps of inspired action that you could take in the next seven days that would help you to do something out of your comfort zone? What are ways that you need support to move through this process emotionally?

4

You Are Not Broken

Close your eyes, breathe in deeply, exhale, and then say this affirmation: *I am whole.*

On my wedding day to Sean in 2013, we had traveled from Australia to Las Vegas for the special event. We had booked a beautiful resort, all our friends and family were there, and the setting was magical. I had carefully packed my wedding dress but needed to send it to the local dry cleaners so that they could steam the wrinkles out of the white tulle skirt. Hours before I was to walk down the aisle, I removed the plastic wrapping around the dress, and, to my utter shock, discovered that the zipper had been completely removed! This was a bride's worst nightmare! I had the most exquisite dress that had been tailored to my body, and now it was broken. I remained calm. Actually, it was very uncharacteristic of me to be so calm in such a moment of chaos. I knew that there was no benefit to arguing with reality, so I started to think who could help. Thankfully, my lady of honor, Dallyce, and also my dad always traveled with a sewing kit. Dad was always great with repairs and stitching the hems on my school dresses, so I knew he was the right person to sew me into my dress. It took a little over one and a half hours of Dallyce threading the white cotton and Dad making careful stitches with the needle that would look natural on the back of my bridal gown. I will cherish this memory of devotion, support, and dedication for the rest of my life. Something that was broken, or felt so broken, actually turned out to be the most beautiful blessing in disguise.

TURNING YOUR PAIN INTO POWER

The most exquisite lotus flower can grow in the muddiest of puddles, and you can always make lemonade when life gives you lemons. This reminds us of the opportunity in pain, suffering, inconvenience, or sadness to rise up and believe beyond what we can see. Something beautiful is usually on its way—connection, awareness, consciousness, and wholeness. So whatever you're currently going through right now—whether you are facing illness, you can't pay your bills, something you love is lost, or you are experiencing trauma from your past that is hurting your heart, please remember: you are not broken. The more you embrace remembering that you will be okay, the higher you rise and the faster you heal. You are not broken. It may feel that way, but it's about trusting that your sense of self goes through cycles just as the seasons change from winter to spring. Your pain always has the option to turn into power.

I used to think that being broken or having a story of suffering was like wearing a badge that would lead to being more accepted by people. I used to think that being destructive or rebellious was an act of personal expression—like when I created that batch of fake vomit that I mentioned in chapter 2. Or when I vandalized a bus stop or completely dead-headed all the prize-winning daisies from the house of a cheerleader girl I hated. The truth is that I was looking for love and belonging. This is quite often from where feeling broken and making foolish choices with unintended consequences stems. We deflect our pain onto others or seek approval in unconventional ways.

As an example, each day back in 1993, I took the bus to school. I was at an all-girls' school, and we shared a bus with the local boys' school. This was awesome because we got to see boys, and it was somewhat of a treat to connect with members of the opposite sex. There was this one boy on the bus named Leo. He had the band name *Metallica* written in bubble writing on the bottom of his schoolbag. He had long brown hair and brown eyes and wore tattered friendship bands around his wrist. The boys were held to the same strict uniform standards as the girls; however, Leo looked scruffy, with a crooked tie, without his shirt tucked in, and I loved it. The only thing was that he was seventeen, and I was just thirteen. I really hoped with every ounce of my soul that Leo would sit next to me on the bus ride home each day. When he did, we would speak about so many interesting things, and he really felt like a kindred spirit. I would sketch pictures of skulls and flowers and he would comment on how good my drawings were and how they would make rad tattoos. This was probably a very basic attention-seeking strategy since I was unaware how to flirt or get the attention of a boy. Leo had a heart of gold. He was kind, and sweet, and we would chat about heavy metal bands we liked, and I would sell him cigarettes that I'd stolen from my parents. I know, it sounds bad. My parents smoked like chimneys and stockpiled so many cigarettes that they didn't know how many they smoked each day, but one was always alight. I thought that I was doing them a health favor and making a little money on the side. I kept the stolen cigarettes in a tin that had pictures of kittens on the side of the box. The metal kept the smell of tobacco pretty undetectable, which I believed was a stroke of genius.

I knew in my heart that there was no hope of Leo wanting me to be his girlfriend anytime soon and that he just saw me as a little sister. However, then the day arrived that I had been hoping for. He handed me an invitation to celebrate his eighteenth birthday at his house. I was so overwhelmed with excitement and anxiety that my stomach hurt. There would be no way my parents would allow me to go, and I wasn't even going to ask them. My meticulous plan was to have my friend Beth stay over for the night. We would go to bed early, stuff our beds with toys, climb out the window, and walk five kilometers (or three miles) in the pitch darkness of the night to the party. And that's what we did. The country roads were unlit, and so every time a car drove past, we hid behind a tree. Beth and I were just thirteen years old, but this was the most exciting thing we had ever done in our lives, and it was thrilling. We arrived at the party, and I handed Leo his gift. I'd made him a drawing and bought a mini lava lamp, and then he hugged me! He. Hugged. Me. That was it; I wanted to marry him at that moment. There were teenagers everywhere making out, dancing, and drinking beer. Beth and I were just keeping to ourselves, and then I saw a familiar pair of headlights charge down the driveway. My dad drove a 1977 baby-blue Daimler, and it had a very distinguishable sound and round headlights. I heard that sound, and I felt like I was going to be sick. I knew my dad had found us. The door slammed, and he marched over to me with the full force of his anger and concern.

"What do you think you're doing with my daughter?" my dad said to Leo. He was pointing right at his face. Poor Leo had no clue what was going on, as most of the kids that shared the same bus route with us were invited to the party.

"And you? *You* are going to boarding school, young lady!" He was fuming with rage.

Apparently, he had found the invitation to the party that I had kept in my cigarette tin with the kittens on it.

Beth and I got in the car feeling very remorseful, and my dad drove us home. We were in big trouble. I felt so embarrassed, and I felt broken. All I wanted to do was spend time with this cute older boy, and I had no idea it would land him in such trouble.

The next evening, Leo and his parents called my dad to apologize. It was the right thing to do, and I believed it showed amazing character. I innocently didn't have any understanding that being friends with an older boy would get me into so much trouble. We remained friends for a while, but all my actions showed Leo was that I was a sad little girl, which is how I felt. This is the kind of experience that shapes a person and sets the stage for either empowerment or disempowerment.

There is no way in the world I would allow my children to have done something like this! I made foolish decisions from believing I was broken and entitled—a most dangerous pairing. This could have also been a potentially high-risk situation with many unknown variables. I was naive and only thinking of myself. If I could share advice with thirteen-year-old me, it would to have been to make honesty the best policy and to have had some kind of awareness of the potential hazards of the situation.

MISTAKES DEFINE YOU AND GATHER WISDOM OVER TIME

You see, life is seasonal. It's an ever-changing, ever-evolving playground of spiritual lessons that sometimes energetically beats us up and then leaves us wondering what the heck happened. I get sent messages all the time from people who feel as if they have hit rock bottom and are not sure how to rise above their feelings of fear to climb their way out of the ashes. Each and every time I get these messages, I like to remind the writers to give themselves permission to feel. No more sweeping it under the rug and pretending it's not important and not there. Feel those feelings, and show up for them with compassion and trust. Compassion, so you can be gentle on yourself. And trust that your emotions are moving their way through your life experience in the way that they need to so you can heal and grow.

As an example, a young woman asked me a question on social media to give her a sign as to whether or not her partner was cheating on her. I responded saying that no sign was required. I instructed her to have a conversation with the guy expressing how she felt and stating that honesty and integrity are important to her. I also added that if he was being unfaithful, she must not label herself as broken like there is something wrong with her. Blaming ourselves only creates depressive feelings.

When I was living on welfare and I'd first moved into my tiny apartment in 2009–2010, I was wrestling with depression on a daily basis. Each morning when I woke up, my eyes would open and I could feel the pillow behind my head. There would be a sense of dread in the pit of my stomach because I didn't feel like facing another day. In those moments, I had a choice as to how the day would unfold and the feelings I would bring to it. I could either allow the fear to win, or I could get my butt up out of the bed and do whatever it took to make sure that my children didn't realize how much of a scary situation we were facing. Thomas and Olivia were my *why*—they were my reason for wanting to be better and wanting to understand how I could be the best emotionally empowered version of myself. There was no more space in my life to stay stuck anymore. I was thirty years old, and I'd never truly experienced the freedom of being an adult out in the world on my own. It was super scary—better late than never, I guess—and I was ready to fly. One of my rock-bottom moments was when I had less than forty cents to feed my children for two days. I ended up buying a no-name bag of pasta. I've told this story a million times over the last ten years in podcasts, interviews, and onstage. I had a bottle of ketchup and a bag of pasta, and my babies went to bed with full bellies for just forty cents. When you live in a humid climate without a refrigerator in your home, then the food gets moldy quite easily. I couldn't afford to waste anything at that point. What I've never admitted publicly before is that one evening, I scraped the green fuzzy mold off the end pieces of a loaf of bread, and that's what I ate for my dinner. I toasted it, sprinkled it with a little salt and pepper, and ate the moldy crusts. I would often skip meals so my children could eat. And I was so stubborn that I never asked my parents to help out because they had their own lives to take care of, and, foolishly, I felt like I had something to prove. If I asked for help, it would burst the illusion of success that I was always trying to radiate out into the world.

When I left my marriage in 2009, I had over $30,000 worth of student debt that shouldn't have been in my name, but it was. The bank seemed to call me every other hour to ask when they could expect my next payment to be made. Once I recognized the numbers, I started avoiding the calls. My mindset was trapped with impoverished thinking at the time because I truly believed that I had no hope of ever paying the debt back to the bank. One of my only options was to file for bankruptcy, which I nearly did twice. At that point in my life, I had to get real with myself about how I could stop feeling so broken and defeated by life. I wanted to attract abundance or at least financial stability. I wanted to attract true love and connection with another human being. I wanted to provide a safe, healthy, and happy environment for my children. I felt like Humpty Dumpty, the anthropomorphic egg from the famous English nursery rhyme:

Sarah Prout sat on a wall,
Sarah Prout had a great fall.
All the king's horses and all the king's men
Couldn't put Sarah together again.

But it wasn't anyone else's responsibility to do that. It was mine! I didn't need horses or men; I needed my own plan of action and to rescue myself once and for all. One thing is for sure, the seasons of our lives are given to us as a way for our consciousness to expand and our souls to remember who we truly are and what we are capable of achieving. Transitions in life happen to everyone—no one is immune to riding out the wave of the uncertainty of how the next chapter of one's life will unfold. Most of the time, these transitional phases are completely beyond our control. Breakups, divorce, death, loss, miscarriage, illness, hardship, and a multitude of other divinely planned trials and tribulations are all instances that call our souls to move into a new level of awareness, sovereignty, and ultimately strength.

IT'S NORMAL TO FEEL BROKEN SOMETIMES

When you give in to the notion that you are broken in some way, then you must stop to examine how you feel. Ask yourself, *What is going on in my heart right now? And what do I need to feel supported?*

Making permanent decisions based on temporary feelings is one of the most dangerous things we can do as human beings. But when we remember that life never stays the same, then we embrace our own inner capacity to change. Here are five things to help you to remember to lean into wholeness:

1. **You are always changing:** As humans, it's impossible not to change and transform as life unfolds. No one stays the same for the duration of their lifetime, which is a wonderful realization.

2. **Your character matures and evolves over time:** When I think back to some of the decisions and choices that I made when I was younger, I know I would never

make them now! Maturity is a gift that comes with time, environment, community, and experience.

3. **Painful experiences teach us how to behave:** Once you know something is painful, it's usually the best thing to avoid doing it again. When my son, Thomas, was two, I told him not to put his hand near the steam iron because it was hot. He did it anyway—which was the first and last time he did it.

4. **The past does not define the future:** We are not the sum of our past choices, mistakes, or experiences. We are the sum of the awareness and the clarity we can bring to the present moment.

5. **We live in an infinite Universe of infinite possibilities:** We do! When we rise above judgment of ourselves and others and show up with compassion, then our magnificent potential is revealed.

KARMIC DEBRIS AND GETTING LUCKY

Karma is based on the notion that the energy you put out there will always return to you. Karma is a much more advanced concept than just reincarnation and attracting so-called bad karma. As spiritual beings having a physical experience, it's hard to believe that when we are born into the world we might have some sort of karmic debt to pay back over the course of our lifetime.

What we do have, however, is the collective impact of generational and ancestral wounds. The generations that have lived before us might have inadvertently passed down some of their most limiting beliefs to us. We store these nuggets of knowledge and wisdom in our cells, in our energy centers, and in our beliefs that we hold about life and how it works.

But what would happen if you were prepared to go head to head or toe to toe with the karmic debris or possibly even lifetimes of your soul's evolution? What would it feel like to release the tension of limitation that you might not even have been aware you have been carrying since the moment you were born? Rest assured you have the power to clear the energy and the cellular memory from your body. And it all begins with intention. Even just by asking those questions, you open up that beautiful heart of yours to the essence of infinite wisdom to clear the karmic filing cabinet of baggage.

When you do this, you become magnetic. You start to facilitate deep healing where you can replace beliefs of scarcity and unworthiness with new and vibrant beliefs of abundance and hope. You can unlearn old patterns and assumptions that no longer serve you. Many people out there hold the belief that they are either lucky or unlucky, and it's simply not true. With the responsibility that you hold in your gut and in your heart to interpret your intuition, it's important that you remember that you create your own luck by discerning your own path forward. Each moment offers an emotional response and guides your way home to remind you that you are not broken.

RECURRING HEARTBREAK AND BREAKING POINTS

"If you carried her to full term, she probably would have died within the week. Sometimes Mother Nature is kind." The doctor handed me a tissue because I was crying so much after receiving this news. She was as compassionate as possible given the familiarity of the situation.

It was early 2014, and I was getting the results back from the fertility specialist clinic that took DNA samples from the tiny body that I'd carried for nearly ten weeks in my womb. It was only five weeks earlier that I was rushed to the emergency room. I needed to use the restroom, and the nurse handed me a brown paper bag to collect what was painfully passing through me— blood clots the size of baby carrots and small lumps of flesh.

The doctor explained that my baby had a condition known as trisomy 18. I still would have carried her for as long as I could despite the odds stacked against any likelihood of her survival. And during this visit to the fertility doctor, I was told I was pregnant yet again but that it wasn't going to be successful. This was miscarriage number four, and the emotional pain of loss was continuously unbearable. I should have given my body a break, I should have shown myself more compassion, but I felt like a failure.

So while sitting in the office getting news of why the last pregnancy failed, I still had questions as to why the current baby I was pregnant with failed to grow yet again.

There wasn't a heartbeat, and my body needed a little help to understand that it wasn't pregnant anymore. The doctor sent me home with a pill called *misoprostol*. I'd wash the pill down with a giant glass of water and within an hour my body would start cramping to release the leftover pregnancy tissue yet again.

I went up to my room with three candy bars and a stack of glossy magazines and told Sean not to come in unless I said it was okay. As soon as I started to cramp, the pain felt excruciating. With each contraction, I felt like my heart was breaking a little more. The loss felt like full-blown labor pains paired with excruciating pangs of grief.

"Where are you? Where are you? Where are you?" I was sobbing on the side of the bathtub and pleading with the soul of my baby to stay with me. I could feel her presence. I didn't understand how at my age (thirty-three at the time), I could keep getting pregnant so easily and yet these heartbeats kept dying within me.

I felt so broken, so alone. God and the Universe had abandoned me.

At some point throughout life, we've all been there. Collapsed in the corner of our own upset emotions and feeling hopelessly broken without knowing how to make things better. We often experience an upsetting concoction of sadness, self-pity, and self-loathing at the same time. The key thing to remember is that feeling broken is not only inevitable but also normal, and it's okay. We all have history, stories, and baggage to process—sometimes when we least expect it. It usually helps to remember that you will be okay as time passes.

TRAUMA AND SEEKING APPROVAL

The residual trauma from having recurrent miscarriages reacquainted me with other times in my life when I'd felt broken. There were so many experiences that changed me over the years where I was activating my people-pleasing tendencies. It was this silent undercurrent that was consistently being repressed over and over again. In my early adulthood, I didn't believe that I had experienced any major trauma at all. My parents often told me that kids were starving in other places and walking miles upon miles to find clean drinking water. Yes, this was important for the sake of gaining perspective, but it didn't honor and validate my feelings in the times I needed a space to express myself if I felt that something was wrong. With the rise of the #MeToo movement on social media in 2017, I started having memories reemerge from my childhood that I had chosen not to think about. I didn't believe that anything truly "bad" happened to me, but I started having flashbacks of possibly being groomed by a child predator when I was in elementary school, or *primary school*, as it is known in Australia.

A man in a position of authority was a little too friendly when I was asked to help out in the school office on a regular basis. I would see him stand outside of the classroom and then knock on the door to interrupt our math class.

"Sarah Prout, I need your help." He would point at me, wave for me to join him, and smile.

My classroom teacher nodded to say it was okay. Each time this happened, I beamed inside because I felt special and chosen. My face would blush, and it would soon pass as I would follow the man up to the administration office, where he would close the door behind us. My regular task was to sort and staple the stack of paper newsletters that were to be distributed to the children of the school. He would often rub my shoulders and my eleven-year-old chest and tell me to relax because I was too tense. I remember my body stiffening, as I knew that this kind of physical contact was not okay and he was crossing some serious boundaries. I didn't have the necessary assertive communication skills to tell him to stop. In a really twisted way, I also didn't want to say anything that would make him not want me to be there for him anymore. I had no idea that boundary-crossing dynamics like this could form my upcoming people-pleasing behavior that would last for decades.

I never told anyone about this experience because I took pride in being the "reliable one" that had a special job to do in the office. I think as I'm writing these words, I just figured out where I first attached seeking love to an addiction to achievement.

I didn't tell my parents about my experience at school until many years later because I couldn't be 100 percent sure that there were actual sinister intentions behind his actions. I still can't be sure. There is always the option that he was a well-meaning man, but the fact that he would single me out of the classroom on a regular basis and ask me to help seemed to be all the classic warning signs of grooming. I was vulnerable, trusting, and always eager to please, even if it was just by stapling a stack of paper newsletters.

Every time I was agreeable, people-pleasing, and seeking approval, I was suffocating my soul with each decision to say yes. This pattern stayed with me until I was in my thirties, and it ranged from saying yes to various boyfriends, to rushing around to find socks when my husband was arrested on that fateful night in May 2009. I was also not comfortable being alone, which is why there is such a dominant pattern of seeking male approval in this book.

Trauma manifests for people very differently, and what's very important to remember is that it's not your fault and there is no shame in seeking help and emotional support.

I am a very passionate advocate for the power of therapy in conjunction with holistic practices to facilitate healing.

Now I measure healing and success based on the amount of joy I feel on a daily basis that I can share with a true partner in life who loves me no matter what and who I can be myself around without the pressure of proving my worth.

All three of our daughters—Olivia, Lulu, and Ava—have practiced the martial art known as tae kwon do. One of their core principles is to embody this phrase and philosophy:

Self-esteem is the joy of being myself.

Every time I hear this or hear them say this statement, it makes me feel like I'm going to cry. It's a powerful reminder that feeling broken is the journey back to seeking the joy of being yourself. The best part is that you don't need anyone else to do this.

BE GENTLE AND KIND TO YOURSELF WHEN IT COMES TO NEGATIVITY

As I've said, it's normal to feel broken sometimes. And when we do go through these tough seasons, it's important to turn to our friends and family for support and comfort to ease the pain. The personal development industry and self-help space does extremely powerful work for humanity. I feel incredibly blessed in my line of work to help empower others to manifest their best lives. However, there can be slight pressure or focus in the industry when it comes to processing negativity. Sometimes it can be encouraged to be swept under the rug. If you're around someone negative, then that must lower your vibration and cancel all your intentions with the Universe. So it's best to avoid negative people, especially people that are emotionally suffering, right? Protect your energy field at all costs! Let's judge them, talk about how hooked in their stories they are, cut the cord, and sage the crap out of our auras. Nope. This is not the right or most compassionate approach. The best attitude to carry around in your heart is compassion— not only for others but for yourself. The bottom line and the golden thread that binds us all is that we are all living, breathing human beings. We all crave the same intrinsic comforts to stay alive. Having bad days or cycles of fearful thoughts is normal because you are human.

So next time you think of assuming that things are a certain way, stop, pause, and cultivate the awareness that there is always so much more behind the perception of a story. And energetically, you always become the energy of that which you judge. When you embrace the wholeness of human expression and don't try to spiritually bypass the lessons being presented to you, then you master the art of true empathy.

I adore the Japanese art form known as *Kintsukuroi* or "golden joinery," in which broken pottery (such as mugs and bowls) is repaired with powdered gold and lacquer to fill the cracks. These repaired pieces of pottery are far more valuable and cherished once they have been through this restorative process. You are no different.

I SEE YOU

I was at a personal development retreat in the Dominican Republic in 2013. Sean and I flew from Australia and counted this trip as part of our honeymoon. It was mid-November, and only a few weeks earlier, we had an ultrasound appointment to discover a healthy baby with a healthy heartbeat. The doctor said it would be fine to travel, and so I found myself in a tropical paradise with the time and space to work on myself for once. The motivational speaker on the stage gave the audience a task. We had to walk around the room, lock eyes with other people, and say, "I see you." I can't even tell you how confronting this was for me. I wanted to hide. I wanted to pull up my walls and not let anyone in. I felt naked, vulnerable, and in no way ready to hold eye contact with a total stranger. I could barely even share this level of intimacy with Sean. For years, when I was married to my first husband, I felt unseen. I had trained myself to feel comfortable flying under the radar and to be invisible. This exercise was pushing me to the boundaries of my comfort zone, and as soon as it was over, I breathed a sigh of relief but knew I had a problem. My heart started to hurt.

That evening, there was a party on the beach. The event organizers had created beautifully decorated tables on the sand overlooking the magnificent Caribbean shoreline. I got dressed up and loved the feeling of not wearing shoes to a dinner party. I didn't have anyone to look after, I wasn't on mommy duty, and it was one of the first times in my adult life where I was truly starting to relax. I remember getting up from the table because I needed to use the bathroom. It was dark in the stall, but I looked down to see blood in my underwear. Again, my heart started to hurt. I was so far away from home. I didn't have travel health insurance. I also knew that the bleeding would probably become unmanageable within twenty-four hours. I rushed out of the bathroom to find Sean. Out of hundreds of people, he instantly looked up at me and we locked eyes; he must have sensed something was wrong.

"I'm bleeding," I said quietly.

He whisked me away to our hotel room so we could plan our next moves. I wanted to go home, but it would be at least seventy-two hours before I could be back on Australian soil. Our beautiful friend Dawn spent over an hour trying to change our flights to leave Punta Cana as soon as possible. The only option was for Sean and me to spend a day in New York before we could fly home. It felt like my body was keeping the hope alive that my baby was okay, but there was no way of truly knowing. We had to remain as present as we could with one another until we could finally have the confirmation we needed.

We made our way to the hospital, to the emergency ultrasound machine.

"I'm not seeing a heartbeat. Maybe it's just too early to see," the technician expressed sympathetically.

It wasn't. At nearly ten weeks, my baby had stopped growing. I felt so broken at the time and had no idea that the broken feeling would multiply with each upcoming loss. It was like the Universe was punishing me in some way. And then it occurred to me that if I wasn't comfortable in my body, then why would a baby want to grow in there? This was flawed thinking inspired by deep shame.

There is no amount of shame that is carried that cannot be undone by the power of love and a little bit of self-awareness. Our minds quite often push things away that don't feel good, and when this happens over an extended period of time, we can become shut down or closed off from the beautiful, magical landscape of nourishment that our hearts have to offer us. I have a tiny heart tattooed on my right wrist. It's a reminder to make the journey from my head to my heart because so often I forget.

UNPACKING MORE BAGGAGE

I've covered so many themes so far, such as the emotional pain of my miscarriages to the anguish of seeking safety in relationships and the dysfunction that happened along the way. When I am working with my clients and students who are experiencing various hardships in their lives, I like to remind them that the Universe is currently writing their life story and that the pain can one day turn into power. Hindsight is such an incredible spiritual gift when you have enough distance from the situation to reflect on what went right and what to avoid next time so you don't repeat the same patterns.

I want you to know that I am reluctant to share the following themes with you because of how deeply personal they are. After working with thousands of people over the last decade, I have seen in action the healing portal that opens up when someone is willing to be truly vulnerable—which is why I'm willing to share. I might as well be letting you stare into my eyes at a personal development conference—which, by the way, after an intense amount of healing, is something I am more than comfortable doing nowadays. With that being said, when it comes to talking about sex (yes, we are going to be talking about sex), I want to travel back with you in my time machine to show you how our sexual experiences can open our hearts to intimacy or leave us feeling broken.

I believe that sex, worthiness, and feeling loved are inextricably linked. Intimacy with another human is so important and vitally sacred. And yet somewhere along the journey for many people, it becomes less magical and even something shameful. It becomes a way to stuff down feelings instead of sharing them in a conscious way. Many people within society are starved of affection and intimacy, or feel lonely because they have yet to find their forever person if they are looking for one. The beliefs we form around sex and worthiness often stem from first experiences that are either wonderful or underwhelming—or both.

So let's track back to my inability to look into other people's eyes. It's so intimate; there's nowhere to hide. And then flash forward into my beautiful marriage to Sean Patrick Simpson. I can proudly say that we are connected in so many ways. Our connection is so strong, and we often joke that we feel as if our bodies were custom made for one another. We lose track of time and space. It was always powerful and sacred in this way, even when I was healing from my past trauma.

It was this way even when I was in deep mourning and grief when my body felt so broken after the miscarriages. It was this way even in times where we felt disconnected and were experiencing tough times emotionally in our marriage. This is why it's so important to find a partner that can hold space for you in body, in mind, and in spirit. More importantly, and this is the crux here, that you are able to hold space for yourself in body, in mind, and in spirit. But when you are with a partner, it takes a willingness to communicate and to explore one another's needs. With that being said, there is a radical difference in who I am now, and who I am becoming, versus who I was as a teenager learning to love and learning how to set healthy boundaries. This is where I would like to illustrate how beliefs get etched into one's psyche.

FLASHBACK TO THE '90S

I have memories of being an awkward teenager at a house party when this guy stuck his tongue down my throat and it really grossed me out. The way it seemed to be working was that boys and girls were pairing up to go outside onto the lawn and make out, or "pash," which is what they called it in Australia in 1995. I had kissed a boy before, but not like this. It was like he didn't really care about who I was and what I had to say. I don't think he even knew my name or bothered to ask me. We had barely spoken, and I found myself flat on my back on the grass with his tongue in my mouth and his body pressed up against mine. It was like the eighteenth birthday party I'd snuck out of the house to attend a few years earlier. All this guy did was tell me that I was cute, hold my hand, and lead me outside under the stars to what I believed was the most romantic of destinies. His kissing felt rough and impersonal as if there should have been space to converse first before taking this first step. His hands kept on trying to make their way to my boobs or into my corduroy pants, but I blocked his repetitive attempts with the precision of an Olympic goalkeeper.

I was such a romantic that as soon as I knew what his last name was, that was going to be my last name too. Remember, I was eager to have my self-esteem validated by someone else loving me. Rob was tall and lanky with brown eyes and blond hair. At sixteen, he'd decided to quit school and spend his time working at the local supermarket stocking shelves.

Even though I was so young at the time, my heart had set a very clear boundary. I had promised myself that I would not have sex with someone without being *mutually* in love. They had to know my soul before I would ever let them near my vagina. I followed Rob around like a lovesick puppy, even lying to my parents about where I was so that I could spend alone time with him. After about two weeks of us pashing on a regular basis, one night he invited me to sneak into his home while his parents were sleeping. I was instructed to keep very quiet and not use the bathroom under any circumstances. He offered me a glass of water, which I accepted and then regretted immensely due to the bathroom rule.

Rob's bedroom was covered in posters of Pamela Anderson sporting her high-cut red iconic *Baywatch* swimsuit. The room smelt like sweaty socks, cheap deodorant, and unwashed sheets with the distinct musk of puberty. To my utter surprise, Rob had a waterbed! If you really need to pee and you have to sleep in a waterbed, it can be extremely uncomfortable. My bladder became my worst enemy, but I was willing to get a urinary tract infection just to sleep in the same bed as this handsome human so that he could profess his undying love for me before we took our relationship to the next level. We pashed for what seemed like hours, and it was like someone was inserting a small kiwifruit in and out of my mouth to obtain some kind of world record. And then when the sun rose, I left, on foot, to find the closest public restroom before I exploded.

That week, Rob started to withdraw. He didn't want to spend time with me anymore. He didn't want to pash me. He didn't return my calls. The next time we were hanging out, I asked him what the matter was and what he needed.

"You know what I need, Sarah Prout? A pair of tits and a CU*T!"

For those of you that aren't familiar with the C-word (or *See You Next Tuesday*), it's a word that can be pretty offensive to most people. Rob said this in front of his friends and in front of my best friend, Kasey, too. My heart broke. I was just a toy—a toy with boundaries that I am really proud of until this day. I wanted love, and he wanted my virginity. Because Rob didn't like me anymore, I felt broken. This could have been a powerful point of choice to have claimed my self-esteem, to Be the Love I wished to feel, and to stop caring so much to be paired up with another human. But it wasn't. My lessons were still being delivered until I was ready to claim ownership of my self-worth.

My mother always told me that boys would only be interested in one thing from me, and it wasn't my quick wit or sense of humor (sadly). This planted the very limited belief in my heart, which meant that I made sex wrong. Even in my first marriage, it felt wrong—like I was doing something I wasn't supposed to be doing. And then being married felt like something that I wasn't supposed to be doing. Having an affair definitely felt like something

I shouldn't have done. And then my first feelings of true empowerment happened when I felt strong enough to stand on my own and file for divorce.

THE PATH FORWARD TO WHOLENESS

Wholeness is embracing the entire story—the beauty, the mess, the mistakes, and the pain. You can move through it into a space of clarity, stillness, and peace. Feeling broken is your call to remember that you can never actually break. You're stronger than a diamond on your own path, and the Universe is guiding you on every step of the journey.

Collective Kindness Exercise 4

Make it a point to make eye contact with people that you encounter during your day— the person at the supermarket, on the bus, at the post office. Say in your mind, *I see you,* and send positive healing energy their way. This not only raises your vibration but raises the collective vibration of humanity as well.

THINGS THAT HELPED ME TO FEEL WHOLE

1. **I allowed myself to feel a full spectrum of emotions:** In the personal development and self-help industries especially, there is a lot of fear of feeling or expressing negative emotions. It could lower your vibration, cancel your manifestations, or make your chakras all fizzle out of alignment. This flawed thinking encourages emotional suppression, which stunts wholeness. I was really great at putting on a brave face, sweeping my issues under the rug, and not talking about the pink elephant in the corner of the room. As I was healing, I would allow myself to feel my feelings— good, bad, and ugly. If I felt like I had a lot of pent-up sadness, I would cry it out. If I felt like I was angry, then I would give myself full permission to express it in a safe way (this took a lot of practice). Our emotions are magical portals to infinite possibilities. When you reveal your feelings, instead of trying to hide them, you can feel truly whole and authentic.

2. **I celebrated special moments and milestones:** One of the most powerful ways that I got through my time living below the poverty line as a single mother was to take one day at a time. Some days were extremely scary when I didn't know if we were going to run out

of money for food or toilet paper or if our electricity was going to get shut off. Reaching the end of each day felt like a milestone. This is where I learned how to practice the art of tiny gratitude. Even if it was just feeling appreciation that my kids had dry toast for dinner and their tummies were full, I knew I had something to feel so grateful for.

3. **I actively leaned into joy:** One of my favorite things to do is to write lists. As simple as it sounds, I would write lists of things that would bring me joy. Joy is a value that I have to live and express every single day. Just like people have habits about brushing their teeth or washing their hands, I have a habit of being joyful. I love to laugh and feel playful, so seeking joy every single day is how I activate and maintain my own magic. It's so simple it might seem stupid, actually. For instance, when I feel my face in the sunshine, it brings me joy. When I cuddle my kids or take the first sip of a hot cup of tea in the morning or feel like dancing to a song I love, it brings me great joy and lights me up. Joy keeps me present, grounded, and lighthearted to navigate the ups and downs of daily life.

4. **I connected with the Universe:** Throughout many times in my life, I have felt so lonely that I sparked a conversation with the Universe. In fact, we formed quite a beautiful relationship. I would ask for help, say

thank you for things, and ask how I could be sent divine guidance or how I could be of service to others in need. The Universe would always respond, every time when I was being intentional. When we connect with the Universe, we recharge our energy systems and lean into the truest essence of who we are as human beings.

5. **I chose between support or solution in my times of need:** Have you ever just wanted to be heard instead of being bombarded with a solution or a quick fix to your problem? Nothing's quite as aggravating as being given unsolicited advice. For instance, when I need to talk to Sean about something that is on my mind or in my heart, he usually asks me if I want support or a solution. Sometimes I say both. Using this point of choice in our relationship allows us to hold space for each other and doesn't allow room for me to feel like his intentions are to fix or solve me in some way, because I'm not broken.

JOURNAL PROMPTS: Be the Love and Know That You Are Not Broken

FEEL: What are things, people, places, and experiences that make you feel whole, cherished, and valued? Have you ever felt broken before, and if so, why and how?

_____

_____

_____

HEAL: What are specific ways that you could choose to consciously accept your reality exactly the way it is right now? What are some thoughts and feelings that rise up when you contemplate that everything is perfect and divinely guided in this very present moment?

_____

_____

_____

REVEAL: What advice would you share with your seven-year-old self? What level of responsibility have you taken for others throughout life? How have you carried others? What level of responsibility have you taken for your own emotional reactions to people and experiences?

_____

_____

_____

5

The Law of Letting Go

Close your eyes, breathe in deeply, exhale, and then say this affirmation: *I am surrendered.*

One of the most powerful and transformative elements of changing your life is to learn how to let go of the old and make way for the new. Whether it's releasing the energy of the past or getting rid of unwanted belongings, it can be an arduous journey to identify what no longer serves you, but it's tremendously helpful if you are brave enough to step aside from the patterns that can keep you stuck.

The reason it's so important to let go of your past is because every time you dive back into old and painful memories, it means that you are activating the energy and bringing it forward into your present-day experience. Writing this book, for example, required me to open up old wounds and be aware that I have healed from them and that they are not real anymore. It's said that time heals all wounds, but it's not the time that passes that creates healing; it's our capacity to let go of things that no longer serve us on our journey throughout life. As an example, for many years, my eating disorder was a highly toxic and addictive behavior that I had trouble letting go of. When my anxiety would flare up or get triggered, then I would process my emotions by hurting myself.

It's a uniquely powerful rite of passage to move from the mindset of being a victim to being a survivor. The key distinction between the two is being willing to do the healing work required to keep moving forward in your life despite the pain.

The beautiful snow would pile up on my apartment balcony when I lived in Gothenburg, Sweden, in 2004. I was so far away from my family in Australia, and the only people I had to talk to were my three-year-old son, Thomas, and my husband, who was out of the house for up to fifteen hours a day. I would carefully plan my binges. The moment I heard my husband leave, I would get Thomas ready into his snowsuit, and we would walk to the local candy store. *Godis* is the Swedish word for candy, and I learned that very early on. The river was completely frozen over in winter, and occasionally, we would spot interesting things under the ice, such as bottles, hats, and sometimes dead animals. At the candy store, I would buy two pounds of soft candy, eat it, and then throw it up when my son was sleeping. After each purge, I felt better and brighter. I felt in control until I didn't. I suffered from bulimia that was triggered by my inability to surrender, to let go, and to love myself. I had a small purple journal, and on December 13, 2004, these were the thoughts on my mind that I penned to paper:

> *I feel so awful. Not that I want to affirm that, but why do I feel so terrible all the time? It's been three months since I had a period. I'm not pregnant, but I'd really like to be. I chew my nails all the bloody time and I don't want to. How can I stop? I think I must have no respect for myself whatsoever. I'm mean to my husband, I'm mean to my son, I hate my body, I'm never motivated long enough to achieve anything. I am a sack of shit. I'm so depressed, I need sunlight. I'm only 25 and would really love some friends my own age. I want a life filled with sunshine, and friends, and challenges and laughter. I fucking hate myself and how I'm so fucking lazy. I want to go home.*

You know in your heart and in your gut when it's time to move on and forge a new path for yourself and to ultimately let go. I was tired of pretending that things would get better in my marriage. I was tired of hurting myself with the binges and the lack of self-responsibility. When the pain gets bad enough, you are always forced to create a change or one is created for you. As I wrote in chapter 3 about moving outside of your comfort zone, I wasn't truly ready to create change for myself until 2009.

However, I had to be ready to make a final decision to change. Life is filled with so many "last times," and quite often, we don't even realize it. There will be a last time you are able to pick up your children before they are too big. There will be a last time you kiss your lover, say goodbye to your parents, or pet your beloved dog or cat. Those are the positive things—as sad as they may seem. There are also last times when you choose not to press the self-destruct button and instead select compassion and choose to Be the Love. There was a last time I chose not to respond with violence in an argument. There was a last time I chose to nourish myself instead of activating the cycle of bingeing and purging. There was a last time I stopped feeling bad about myself. The key is to always allow the space for you to get out of your own way and choose the path of peace and self-compassion.

STEPPING ASIDE FOR THE SAKE OF GROWTH

When I briefly moved from Las Vegas to the Hamptons in New York in 2020, my nineteen-year-old son,

Thomas, decided he wanted to stay behind. It was completely understandable because he had a great job, was enrolled in school, and had a very close circle of friends he didn't want to leave. I made the choice very early on not to take it personally. However, the months leading up to our big family move required me to let go in a way that I never had experienced before. For nearly half of my life, I had been raising, nurturing, guiding, and protecting Thomas, and now it was time for us to not live under the same roof anymore. Remember in chapter 2 when I told you about the dream that I had before he was born? It felt like our timeline together spanned way before this physical reality of mother and child. After thirty-four hours of pushing him out of my body, the doctor plonked this little being on my chest. His eyes were open, and he was staring at me like he'd known me for a while. I had this tiny hand wrapped around my pinkie finger, and it didn't feel like he ever wanted to let go. We were, and will continue to be, connected forever.

I felt like this empowering yet swift departure into adulthood was completing some kind of karmic cycle in a way, but at the same time, it was like ripping off a Band-Aid. I'm sure many parents out there feel or felt the sting of letting go of their grown-up babies when they choose to leave the nest. I didn't anticipate that it would hurt my heart in a really primal and cellular way. It felt like deep grief and release at the same time that I didn't see coming. I also want to honor Thomas here, because it was extremely difficult for him too.

In July of 2020, I became very ill with suspected COVID-19. I had the worst headache I'd ever had in my life, and I completely lost all sense of taste and smell. It was all the usual symptoms that had been outlined in the media, and I was very scared that it would escalate into a much more problematic health issue with my lungs since I'd had pneumonia in the past. Thankfully, it didn't get worse. I'd been self-isolating away from the rest of my family in my office for ten consecutive days. I didn't want to take any risks. And although I really missed hugging my kids, it felt like the most responsible course of action to stay away from them while I waited for my test results. In the evenings, in conjunction with feeling exhausted from the headaches and all the body pains, I felt my anxiety begin to rise to a whole new level. Since we were actively looking for a place to rent in the Hamptons, this meant that I had to be truly ready to process the emotions of the change in our family dynamic even though I felt so excited by the upcoming move. One evening, I told Sean that I could feel a panic attack about to happen. With the whirlwind of change, I usually have heightened emotions and need to be extremely self-aware of when the storms of concern appear on the horizon of my heart. Sean asked if I was physically strong enough to go downstairs and place my feet in the pool. I could barely see. The air was warm. My head hurt. The ground was spinning. I could feel my heart racing at what felt like a million miles per hour, and my breathing was shallow. I plunged my feet into the cold water and began to shake and hyperventilate.

Sean kept saying, "You're safe, love. You'll be okay. You're safe, love. You'll be okay."

"I don't want to leave Thomas," I sobbed.

"Love, he's choosing to stay. He'll be visiting us as often as he can and wants to." Sean is always great at offering support and a solution at the same time.

I was releasing some serious energy over the fear of allowing my child to leave the nest. I had no idea that this kind of event would cause such sheer panic in my heart. My guess is that it was some kind of residual trauma from my past. My panic attack felt like it was a release bubbling up—the very visceral experience of entering into a new phase of awareness. When the emotional storm passed, I began to feel better, and I began healing from the virus. I also felt more capable and better prepared to let go. What I didn't realize is that this was just phase one.

I trusted that Thomas had all the emotional resources he needed to be perfectly fine in the world out on his own. He was actually way better off than I had been only eleven years earlier when I divorced his father. It's a sacred rite of passage to facilitate an empowered departure from the family nest. When I was just twenty-four,

I left Australia to live in Sweden, and it was hard being so far away from my parents, but ultimately, I needed that time to grow up and find my own footing.

THE PAIN OF NOT LETTING GO OF YOUR EMOTIONS

I believe that the isolation of the pandemic lockdowns prompted my swift decision to try living in the Hamptons for a while. It was partly due to yearning for more excitement out of Las Vegas and a need for a change of scenery.

We moved our entire household, minus Thomas, to begin our new life in September 2020. Our rented house was magnificent. It was only a ten-minute walk to a very private beach. Apparently, the actor Hugh Jackman (a fellow Australian) shared the same beach, and I often visualized what I would say if we ever crossed paths. It never happened, but it probably would have if we'd stayed.

There was a peace and a stillness of living in this new and exciting place that I hadn't experienced since I lived on a ten-acre property when I was a child. East Hampton felt like a cross between the English countryside and parts of Australia that I missed so dearly. At night, the trees would whisper to one another, and the sky was unlike anything I'd ever seen. The stars were magnificent, and I would often stand on our bedroom balcony at night and get lost in the beauty of the wilderness.

I would look up at the stars and ask the Universe to protect Thomas. I would also thank the Universe for the experience of living somewhere new for a change. It was a breath of fresh air and a much-needed energetic shift for Sean, Olivia, Lulu, and Ava and our three dogs.

During this time, I saw more deer and squirrels than people. In fact, I had this game that I played with my children called "the Daily Squirrel" because there was not a day that passed where I didn't see one of those little critters in my front garden from the kitchen window.

By November, it started to get really cold—which wasn't a surprise. Unlike Sweden and the buzzing city vibes that kept me company, there was a stark isolation that sometimes made me feel like I was on another planet. Also, my son felt so distant and was struggling emotionally with his family being so far away. It's a tremendously steep learning curve when your family say they are leaving and you have to figure out how to pay rent and bills and take care of yourself for the first time in your life. I felt a sense of freedom and also a sense of sadness that I had chosen to leave my child—even if he was an adult.

OUT OF ALIGNMENT IN A TIME OF GREAT UNCERTAINTY

On Thanksgiving 2020, I was woken up at 3:00 a.m. by sharp pains in my chest. The stabbing pain would not cease. I literally thought I was having a heart attack and wasn't sure what was happening to me. I waited until 6:00 a.m. to let Sean know that I thought I needed to go to the emergency room in Southampton, which was a forty-minute drive away. These ongoing contractions were the most worrying thing I had ever experienced physically in my life. The drive seemed extra-long and windy down the backcountry roads with the haunting backdrop of the bare trees.

We arrived at the hospital, and I had to say goodbye to Sean as they whisked me into the triage room to get assessed. I didn't know if I'd ever see him again. Every five minutes, the pain intensified, and my anxiety was at an all-time high. I was tested for COVID-19, placed on a drip, given pain medication, and then x-rayed, examined, scanned, and analyzed. Nothing was wrong with me that they could see.

The doctors then wanted to admit me overnight for further testing, and the admissions doctor came in to ask questions. She was a kind and caring woman who knew that I was in a very unstable and overwhelmed state.

"How many children do you have?"

I listed out their names and ages. This felt similar to the time I'd had to list out the names and ages of my children to the police on the night my ex had his drunken episode that resulted in his arrest. Internally, I felt the same way. I was scared of the unknown and worried I would never see my children again.

The doctor then said to me very compassionately that it must be hard being away from my son on the holidays. I started to sob, and she encouraged it. She patted my shoulder and was fully present with my emotional response.

"I don't think you need to be admitted for more testing, Sarah. I think you are having a stress response and your heart hurts. Cry, and let it out. Let it go."

What I realized is that I had been not taking enough time to rest. My output to the world was much greater than the input to myself, and something was a little out of balance and out of alignment. As a spiritual teacher and an entrepreneur, it's so easy to get swept away in showing up for others, more than you show up for yourself. As a mother, I was always placing the emotional needs of my children above myself too, as a way to appease the past. This time, I was internalizing it, and it was manifesting as illness and pain in my body.

It's important to remember to listen to your body when it is sending you messages. For weeks, I had a weird little twitch in my right eye. I thought it was because I hadn't been wearing my glasses as much as I should have been when in front of the computer. And then my ears had a weird buzzing noise because I went to the beach when it was really cold. And then my chest pains started. The message? I was to slow down and feel my feelings—*feel, heal, reveal.* It was a journey back into my heart.

I'm so grateful for this experience to listen to myself and my intuition in a whole new way. I'm also grateful to have experienced the difference between mentalizing self-compassion and actually showing up with compassion to choose a different and more balanced path.

After a few very considered weeks and some other personal issues that unfolded in our life, we made the empowered decision to move back to Las Vegas for a while. We realized that our family needed to regroup and that my energy needed to be more grounded. We were hopeful that one day we would return to the Hamptons when the time felt right.

THE MAGIC PATH OF INTUITION

You've heard me speak of many spiritual concepts so far, such as connection to the Universe, how the law of attraction works, and the magic path of intuition. Now we're going to dive deeper into how, specifically, the process of letting go in your life translates into direct transformation and empowerment. Letting go is a powerful healing modality for you to be the love you wish to feel.

Having said that, letting go is hard, but it's the ultimate act of love. I've had many of my manifesting students write to me over the years and ask how to attract and get back a boyfriend or girlfriend that had left them. Sometimes it's difficult to know what to say, but I usually instruct them to surrender to the process and trust that if you love someone, then you set them free. As humans, we fear letting go more than anything else because it means we venture into the unknown territories of uncertainty. It's tough to let go of identities too. It's the space of surrendering and relinquishing control and arriving at the exact point when you stop arguing with reality and accept what is.

Control tends to show up for many people in many different ways. For instance, micromanaging your spouse sends a very clear signal that you don't believe they are as capable as you are. But when you detach from your desired outcome, you allow the space for infinite possibilities to unfold for you.

The process of surrendering is actually the most powerful and magical component to mastering the human experience. In meditation, one surrenders and lets go. In moments of true presence, one surrenders and lets go. At rock bottom and times of intense crisis, one surrenders and lets go. At the precise point of physical death, one lets go. It's like the Universe has mapped out this singular curriculum for everyone to understand and experience firsthand during the course of their lifetime.

For many couples who decide to part ways, the breakup is usually over control itself, or because of a constant control battle that cannot be neutralized. These control issues typically tend to fall into several categories, such as:

- Money and finance
- Parenting
- Sex, love, and intimacy
- Household duties
- Time management
- Work responsibilities

When these expectations or values are mismatched or there is a power struggle over things, big and small, the tension in a relationship will escalate and be pushed to its limits. That's why it's so important to release the desire to control your partner—because you can't. The magnificent beauty of a relationship is that you learn how to navigate the space between. That space between is constructed of compassion, communication, and supporting your spouse to be the best version of themselves that they can be. You should also do this within your own heart as well, as an independent and sovereign human being. Have you heard the saying that "success leaves clues"? Well, guess what? Surrendering control leaves clues too.

TIP OF THE TONGUE

One way that I like to explain the process of surrendering and getting results is this. Have you ever not been able to reach a word, a name, or a title in your mind? It feels as if it is on the tip of your tongue. Let's just say it's a book that you enjoyed reading and have forgotten the title of. Your mind keeps trying to reach for the title that you just can't remember, and it becomes increasingly more frustrating and annoying. You might say something like this:

"This is really going to bug me. I wish I could think of the title right now."

And then you put it to the back of your mind. You stop fighting and searching for the information and *you surrender.* You let go. You distract yourself with other things. And then guess what happens next when you least expect it? The title appears in your mind. Every time.

Even though this is a well-known psychological phenomenon, it has spiritual implications too. When you let go and surrender, the Universe can deliver your desires into your reality to create healing or closure. You just have to surrender.

SEE THE CYCLES

Everything in life is cyclic and surrenders to a natural process. As much as you could try not to get old and to beat a biological clock, there is no way (currently) to cheat yourself out of one day arriving at death's door. We're born, we live, we die. Plants, animals, stars, tides, and humans are all on the magnificent wheel of life. And when we remember the law of letting go, which I'm about to explain, then we can begin to guide our experience to be more mindful, trusting, and open to all possibilities.

After I turned forty, I started noticing more gray hair appearing on my head. I would initially grab the tweezers and pluck them out before anyone noticed. And then I asked myself what trying to get rid of them says to the Universe. It says that growth must be hidden, ignored, and removed. I love my gray hairs now. Sometimes I cover them up and other times I feel the silver wisdom and the deep honor of getting older. Another thing that some women tend to complain about is how much of an inconvenience having a monthly menstrual period can be. What if we switched our awareness to gratitude for the cyclic wisdom that is held within our bodies? Our bodies are actually vessels for our intuitive faculties. When we forget to surrender to the deep knowledge and spiritual acumen held within our cells, we tend to stifle our progress throughout life. Our cycles are allies that regulate the understanding of how to surrender when we need to.

SWEET SURRENDER

One of my most popular courses is called the Ancient Manifesting Ritual, which has been taken by thousands of people over the years. My manifesting students and clients have utilized it to set powerful intentions to manifest things such as babies, dream homes, job promotions, and soul mates. This process was taught to me originally by my meditation teacher back in 1999. He referred to this as a ritual called "Mind Marvels." I don't want to give away all the juicy secrets of the process here, but what I will say is that the basic idea is to imprint your subconscious mind and surrender to the outcome. The first step is to come up with a statement or a declaration to the Universe. You need to do it as if your intention has already manifested. You then write out the chosen statement fifty-five times for five days in a row.

I have been teaching this process for well over five years now, and there is quite often a learning curve that is accompanied with trying out the ritual. A person is usually drawn to the ritual because they want to manifest, quickly, something that will make them feel better and feel more in control of their lives. Sometimes, they might use a statement like this: "I have now manifested $1,000 by November 1."

The date then comes and goes, and they are left feeling disappointed because they invested a lot of time and energy (as well as hand cramping) trying out the process of this ritual. And then I remind them that it's not about the words, and it's not even about their intentions. What happens with this process of imprinting your subconscious mind is that as you write, it becomes an automatic process. You actively engage in the experience of surrender. What I noticed is that when you write the same thing over and over and over again, just like writing lines on an old-fashioned chalkboard, it becomes almost effortless. And when a person does this, it allows them to truly let go. It releases resistance. And this is the magic of manifesting.

RESISTANCE AND FLOW

Most people sabotage their levels of success by their inability to surrender and let go. Let's take manifesting as an example. Most people set an intention and get super attached to the outcome. They stalk the walls of the Universe for signs of confirmation. They believe that the object of their fixation must arrive in their desired timeline and in the perfect way or else manifesting is definitely a bunch of codswallop. As I'll discuss in chapter 7, everything is energy. However, there are only two categories that energy falls into: resistance or flow. Resistance is generated when you maintain tight and rigid rules and beliefs of control around how your life shows up for you. Resistance is forcing things to happen; it's the essence of control and facing reality with a combative energy of impatience. It has the same frequency as flushing a brick down a toilet. Flow, on the other hand, is the art of letting go. You are truly surrendered and in a state of trust that the Universe will deliver your desires in perfect divine timing. What you resist persists; most of the time, you wish things were different. However, when you go with the flow, you tap into the magnificent stream of infinite wisdom and limitless possibilities. It's fluid and simple and appears in your life with ease and grace.

DECLUTTERING TO CREATE SPACE

When you let go, the Universe reveals to you a new path to follow. Surrendering clears space and invites the energy of newness and infinite wisdom to guide you on your journey. I have watched *Hoarders,* which highlights the suffering that manifests when we are unable to clear space in our lives and let go of things that no longer serve us. Compulsive hoarding is actually a treatable disorder that can be helped with the assistance of trained clinical psychologists and remedial therapy sessions. There are many different levels of intensity with hoarding behavior, but it mostly stems from previous trauma and an inability to let go of the past. The cases that I watched on *Hoarders* depict people that have been living in houses for decades where they had been unable to part with anything, such as empty cat food tins, milk cartons, toilet paper rolls, and even bags of dog poop. Keeping stacks of trash piled up to the roof leads to it being an extremely unhygienic and unsafe place to reside. Now this is a worst-case kind of scenario, but most people tend to hang on to way too much stuff in their lives that they don't actually need. You might be hanging on to clothes that no longer fit you, or gifts that you didn't like and never used, or mementos from an ex-lover that sit in a keepsake box and collect dust.

One of the most empowering exercises you can do is clear your clutter and get rid of (or donate) the things that no longer support you on your path. Energetically, you are clearing out the old to make way for the new. This is a symbolic act of surrender that the Universe will always respond to.

For instance, I had a client come to me asking for advice on how she could attract a soul mate. She was recently divorced and had a kitchen cupboard filled with all her ex-husband's favorite coffee mugs. I told her to either return them to her ex-husband (even though it had been five years since he'd left) or donate them to a local charity organization. I then told her to go out and buy a set of new matching coffee mugs for herself and her new lover. Every morning, she was to make herself a cup of coffee. I told her to visualize that she would be sharing it with her beloved very soon. Sure enough, he arrived in her reality within just three weeks of clearing out the last threads of energy tied to her ex-husband's presence in her life.

Here are some law of attraction ideas for making space for manifestation and activating the law of letting go. This is based on the idea of using active faith and acting as if your desires have already manifested. It's basically like leaping without a net (surrendering), but not being stupid about it.

The New Thought writer Florence Scovel Shinn phrases the process beautifully here:

> True prayer means preparation. Having made
> your demands on the Universal Supply for any
> good thing, act immediately, as if you expected to
> receive it. Show active faith, thereby impressing the
> subconscious mind with expectancy.

By *prayer* here, Florence refers to intention setting. And by *Universal Supply,* she means the Universe, God, Source of Force, and so on.

It's the most potent energy field in the entire Universe that creates and governs everything. The secret is this: When you set an intention or feel a desire that you'd like to manifest, the key is to channel your energy and vibration into the outcome as if it's already happened. You need to "act as if" and be open to all possibilities. This means buying a wedding magazine before you find the man, perhaps buying a fancy key ring before you buy the car, or buying that little black dress before you lose or gain the weight. This activates the energy of expectation in your vibration and helps tremendously.

Here are some tips to create space by surrendering for specific things to manifest into your life:

- **To make space for manifesting ABUNDANCE:** Clear out your purse or wallet. This frees the energy of prosperity and shows reverence for more money to manifest.
- **To make space for manifesting TRUE LOVE:** As I mentioned above, buy a special coffee or tea mug that will be used by your beloved in the not-so-distant future. Or perhaps clear out space for them in your closet or bedroom.
- **To make space for manifesting a BABY:** Select a small item that will be used by the soul baby that you are calling into the world. Start talking to them now and let them know it's safe to arrive

in perfect divine timing. You also must surrender or let go of your own need to control when a child arrives in your life.

- **To make space for manifesting a DREAM HOME:** Get into the feeling space of checking out as many homes as possible that are for sale that you dream of living in. Not only does this raise your vibration, it also matches you to the energy of your intention. Surrender to the possibility that the perfect home will manifest in the perfect time.

DETACH FROM THE OUTCOME

I understand that when you hear "Just let go of your dreams," it might sound counterintuitive to everything you have learned about focus and channeling your energy into what you really want to experience in your life. First, I want you to understand the difference between being in your head versus your heart. Your head has often tricked you into thinking that you really want something—like getting back with an ex or turning the clock back in some way to make peace with the past. The best thing to do is move your attention to things you can do to let the Universe know you are 100 percent serious about transforming your life. I'm going to share with you a few examples of how I used the process of *active faith* to detach from certain outcomes in my life. Please keep in mind that I am not advocating that you do anything silly like quit your job or move out of your home without anywhere to move to. My hope here is that these specific examples show you how I have periodically made a jump without knowing if the net would catch me.

In 2015, Sean and I decided that we wanted to move from Australia to Las Vegas in the United States. We had talked about it, but I felt like there would be too many obstacles to consider it seriously. One hurdle was that my ex-husband might not let me take Thomas and Olivia out of the country. Another obstacle was that our business was still not making enough money, which was required for us to prove that we have a viable business and income to support our family once we landed stateside. Sean, being an American, made the immigration process easier, but there was still a ton of paperwork to file. Sean met with a lawyer who said it could easily take from three to five years for the process to end favorably. As disheartening as this news was, we didn't want to accept this as our reality, so we decided to take leaps of active faith to move the energy in a favorable direction. First, I simply asked my ex if I could move to the U.S. for the sake of the children and for them to have access to more opportunities. He said yes. I sent the paperwork, and he signed it without resistance. I will always be grateful to him for this act of selflessness. The key here is that we surrendered and let go of our attachment to the outcomes.

Next, we had to manage our finances, and so we decided to immerse ourselves into truly learning how to master the art of digital marketing. Sean studied everything he could on how to create successful Facebook ad campaigns and how to build a profitable sales funnel. In our first month, we went from earning around $5,000 to $20,000. We knew that if our success continued for only a few more months, we would have the proof for the U.S. immigration office that we could thrive as new residents. Next, we had to get rid of all our stuff while we waited for the official stamp of approval to receive our green cards. So what did we do? We decided to have a garage sale to sell all our things before we had the official yes.

In August 2015, we had to fly from Noosa, in Queensland, to Sydney to visit the U.S. embassy for the official immigration appointment. After getting all the paperwork in order, getting fingerprinted by the police, medical exams, and the appropriate vaccinations, we were ready to have our fate decided by the simple stamp of a man standing behind a desk. Our names were called, and we were asked a few questions about our income.

The guy said, "How do you intend to support yourself with this number?" He sounded stern, and then he shuffled some papers and took a deep breath.

At this stage, I was standing next to Sean, and we

were holding hands as tightly as possible with Thomas and Olivia.

Sean replied, "We expect this number to increase over the next few months."

And then the man stamped the paper. It was official. We were allowed to move to the United States to begin the next chapter of our lives. Lulu was just six months old, but we didn't care how long the plane trip would be—we were up for the adventure.

Moving forward requires letting go of your need to control the outcome. Being open to all possibilities is where the magic happens. On September 9, 2015, we landed in Los Angeles en route to Las Vegas with three children, three dogs, seven boxes, and a large flat-screen TV. We checked into a hotel, and we were prepared and surrendered to stay there until we could find the perfect house to rent. And we did.

SURRENDERING YOUR IDENTITY— ESPECIALLY AS A PEOPLE PLEASER WHO CARES ABOUT WHAT OTHER PEOPLE THINK OF YOU

It's important to remember that throughout life, we wear many different interchangeable masks and take on many different roles and responsibilities. I've played the following parts in my life:

- Daughter and daughter-in-law
- Sister, half sister, and sister-in-law
- Granddaughter, niece, cousin
- Mother and stepmother
- Wife, girlfriend, and the other woman
- Business owner, entrepreneur, spiritual teacher, writer, speaker
- New Zealander, Australian, immigrant, expat, and, hopefully one day, American

Each role comes with a series of different rules and expectations that all contribute to how you attach meaning to the way you show up in your life. But here's my question for you: Who would you be if you didn't have these kinds of labels? Beyond your name, beyond what you do for a living professionally, beyond your nationality—who would you be?

You'd be a surrendered and sovereign being. Even with the labels, when you give yourself permission to let go of the expectations and identity elements, then you are truly living life on your own terms. On December 16, 2007, I wrote the following entry into my journal:

Oh boy, what a crappy day! Don't let me wallow, please, God! I hand it ALL over to you. No more of this self-indulgent, self-sabotaging, self-destructive,

self-loathing behavior. IT MUST STOP NOW. I
now pledge to myself to act with love, self-respect, and
integrity with all I encounter. This is my gift to myself.
Merry Christmas, Sarah Louise Prout. I give you the
wonderful, amazing, beautiful gift of YOU for YOU
once and for all. Love xo

Little did I know it, but this would be my daughter
Ava Moon's birthday nine years later. This is why I adore
journaling so much—you never know when significant
dates will loop back to you and illuminate your progress.
Transformation always takes place when you are willing
to move on from the labels of your past and remember
your sovereign self.

In my most recent research into how to be the love
you wish to feel, I now understand the importance of
not feeling responsible for others throughout this process. My people-pleasing tendencies meant that I felt an
extraordinary level of obligation to make other people
feel taken care of. I would unintentionally place myself
at the very end of the pecking order. This meant that I
could truly only surrender when I knew that everyone
else would be okay.

Not that I remember, but my very first experience of
being in the world was the feeling of being strangled.
The umbilical cord was wrapped tightly around my
neck, and as my mother pushed, it tightened the noose.

When I finally came out, I was blue due to the lack of oxygen. There was a heavy silence in the room—a long pause—and then finally I let out a cry. My mother told me that she smiled for the first year of my life. This was probably because I was the first child after the pain of relinquishing her first two sons. My identity was to be there to provide love to my parents. I had to learn how to surrender this so I could finally heal, and this is why it was so hard to live away from my son, Thomas.

Remember: it's okay to take detours in your life and to learn from mistakes. Ultimately, it's the journey back to remembering that you must live your life for you and let go of what no longer serves you and cherish the good things/people/places and experiences that contribute to your grounded well-being.

HOW TO TRUST YOURSELF TO LET GO

Self-trust is a courtship like no other—a romance with yourself, if you will. It's about cultivating a solid sense of discernment, and only you can truly know when it's time to let go and move forward.

Feel your feelings, especially in the pit of your stomach. If you feel butterflies, then take a leap of faith. If you feel anxious or cautious, then wait until you have more data and feel more comfortable before you proceed.

When you create boundaries around your decision-making process, it becomes like a sacred art form—and can be mutually supportive when it comes to truly letting go.

On a daily basis, I want you to consciously develop your powers of discernment. When it comes to choosing what to eat, for example, it's a great practice to tune in to the foods you know will serve you the most. Notice what your gut tells you instead of your taste buds. Your gut might tell you that eating a pizza is better than eating a salad that day, and that's okay. The important part is to pause and ask your higher self to guide you to decisions that will empower your journey and serve you in the best way possible. And the key to unlocking your intuition? It's to surrender and let go.

Collective Kindness Exercise 5

Go through the things you no longer use or need, and either donate, sell, or recycle the pieces. You could be making someone else's day by offering up the things that no longer serve you. This helps to circulate the energy of creativity and goodwill to the people who need it most.

THINGS THAT HELPED ME TO SURRENDER AND LET GO

1. **I educated myself:** One of the most empowering things I have done is immerse myself in online education. When I first started my business, I would work, study, and absorb everything that I could about how to build websites, how to create a blog post, how to write and sell an ebook—the possibilities were endless. I was committed to training myself on how to create a business that could share my message with the world, and I trusted that if I didn't know how to do something, the internet was more than capable of helping me figure it out. When I surrendered to the process, it felt more effortless. And it was.

2. **I was willing to do the work even if I would fail:** There's no such thing as being an overnight success. If you see someone you perceive to be at a certain level of prosperity or success, most of the time, it took some serious work to get there, and they definitely would have strengthened their muscles of surrender along the way. When you want to achieve great things in your life, you have to be willing to hustle and let go at the same time. It's striking a balance between intense focus and release. The type of work ethic and your willingness to succeed will thrive if you trust that you are capable of letting go of the reins of

control. Simply put, if you want to succeed at something, you have to be willing to fail.

3. **I trusted my common sense to guide me away from fear:** This might sound oversimplified, but common sense is a skill that some people don't explore that is really great when it comes to the process of letting go. For instance, I know not to put a knife in the toaster because I will electrocute myself. I know not to eat food that has been in my refrigerator for two weeks (especially if it smells funky), because it will likely make me sick. I check both ways before I cross a road. I know how to check the oil in my car, clean up the glass when it smashes on the floor, and how to mend a hole with a needle and thread when there is a tear in a piece of clothing. The best thing to do is make a list of all the things you know you are capable of doing, whether it's a simple task of practicality or being a first responder in an emergency situation. Just like intuition, the more you acknowledge your levels of common sense, the more it will show up for you in your times of need when you might be forced to let go of your desire to control an outcome. Be prepared and you won't be scared.

4. **I let go of my need to be a martyr:** This is a confession of when I used to micromanage certain situations. Sean and I were moving out of our tiny apartment into a much larger home in Melbourne, Australia. Our

business was only just starting to make a bit of extra money, and yet I had my head in the oven, scrubbing furiously, trying to meet the deadline for the move-out inspection. I felt so much anxiety because of my emotions and because of the oven cleaner fumes. I snapped at Sean and was so mad that I had my head in the oven and he was doing nothing. He left for a short while and then returned to inform me he had hired a cleaner for less than fifty dollars because it would show me that just because I could do something doesn't mean that I should. I am aware that not everyone can do this—and we weren't even able to back then—but it stretched my awareness as to what is possible when you allow others to help you. Wearing a martyr badge is annoying and shows an inflexibility to not let go of control. This awareness was a turning point in my ability to ask for help and also to become a team player.

5. **I used the process of creative visualization:** Psychologists and high-performance coaches work with athletes and other notable people to use the process of creative visualization to play out scenarios of success in their mind's eye before a race or an event. This has been documented to increase the likelihood of accomplishment. Ever since I was a child, I would visualize my desired outcome. With maturity and emotional alchemy on my side, it's an even more

powerful tool to use, and it's so simple. Take five minutes to sit in meditation, and then visualize your ideal outcome or what you would like to manifest. Tune in on how this will allow you to feel and go for it! I'll be explaining more about this process in chapter 7, "Everything Is Energy."

JOURNAL PROMPTS: Be the Love and Activate the Law of Letting Go

FEEL: What have you held on to in life that you know that you should have let go of earlier? If you had to place your level of trust in the Universe on a scale of 1 to 10, what would it be and why? Where in your life do you assert the most control?

_____

_____

_____

HEAL: What are some of the feelings you experience when you think of letting go of someone or something in your life and from the past? What do you think that you are creating new space for in your life if you let go of things, people, places, and patterns that no longer serve you?

_____

_____

_____

REVEAL: How does the energy of surrendering manifest into your life? How does it feel? What are some of the ways that you can let go, surrender, and trust that everything will work out for the best?

_____

_____

_____

6

Your Word Is Your Wand

Close your eyes, breathe in deeply, exhale, and then say this affirmation: *I am intentional.*

The theme and title of this chapter is borrowed from an old book title by one of my favorite New Thought authors of all time, Florence Scovel Shinn. She wrote *Your Word Is Your Wand* in 1928 as a sequel to the wildly successful book titled *The Game of Life And How to Play It.*

Always remember how powerful your words are. Your words have the power to create your experience in each and every moment. Whenever you open your mouth to say something is a beautiful opportunity to examine the intention behind what you're trying to say. Are you reserved when it comes to verbally expressing yourself? Or do you just blurt out whatever's on your mind and not really care too much about how it lands? One thing is for certain—don't say stuff you don't mean, and be careful what you wish for. Or better yet, speak only of things you wish to create.

One of my all-time favorite words is *abracadabra*. It dates back to Aramaic times and also in the Hebrew tradition translates directly to "I create as I speak." Meaning, your words hold power to attract you to what you are talking about. You've probably heard people say, "Abracadabra!" during the incantation of magic tricks, but it holds and embodies a very sacred significance to manifest healing powers.

When you become more intentional with your levels of communication, you will all of a sudden notice how you have the power to guide conversations and relationships with others. I remember when I first started to study language patterns, I noticed that almost everyone around me was stuck in a mode of complaining as a means to converse.

"Oh, isn't the weather miserable?" Insert heavy sigh here.

Years ago, I made a commitment to sharpen my ways of communicating with other people. I wouldn't complain for the sake of complaining or conversing. I would aim to raise my vibration by only speaking the things I wanted into existence. However, this can be venturing out of the world of compassion into the world of spiritual bypassing. Meeting people with kindness is the most important thing to remember when learning about the power of our words to create our reality.

WORDS AS MAGNETS

First, you make a promise to yourself that you're going to rise above the negative patterns of others, offer compassion, and not let their energy affect you. It can only affect you if you allow it. Second, you stand guard at the doorway to your own thoughts and reframe all notions of resistance, rigidity, and negativity and turn them into something softer and more manageable. And third, you learn to listen to yourself, take responsibility for what you say, and trust that you are creating with your spoken word.

When you start to recalibrate your old patterns verbally, it can radically begin to change the world around you. Happy stuff attracts happy stuff, and crappy stuff always attracts more crappy stuff. It's very simple. So next time you're about to have a grizzle about something, remember that your word is your wand. You have the power within you to course-correct.

WIELDING THE WOUNDS IN RELATIONSHIPS

Just as you have the power to create with your words, you also have the power to wound someone with them. It is in our relationships with others that we learn the best, most effective ways to communicate. You've probably heard this saying before:

> Sticks and stones will break my bones, but names will never hurt me.

This statement is simply not true. The words that you choose to use can either contribute to a relationship or they can contaminate it like someone putting a turd in a punch bowl. The reality is that most people walk through life and are completely unaware of how their choice of words and mode of communication affects others.

Before I knew that my mother had given up her first two sons for adoption, I used to say to her when I was younger, "I wish you'd given me up for adoption!" I would say it in anger. I had no idea of the deep and secret wound I was activating and how ridiculously tactless and cruel this would have felt to her. I was playing out the hormonal storm of being a teenager and believing that the rules in our household were extremely unfair. So I turned to having a poisonous tongue as a means to lash out. It's not kind, and it's not conscious. Once I learned the truth of my mother's situation, I never spoke those words again. However, over the years, I have definitely had the capacity to say cruel and mean things in the heat of the moment. This is part of the reason I feel qualified to share this with you—I have had to do a lot of unlearning over the years to retrain myself to be more conscious with the words I choose to use.

When we start to feel hurt, one of the quickest emotional fixes to approach conflict is to say mean and potentially harmful things as a form of retaliation. Being in attack mode or being defensive with your line of communication is like wielding a sword. If you're not careful, you can puncture a vital organ—like the heart. The hurtful words stick in the crevices of someone's soul and change the way they behave. And sometimes these modes of communication can be so subtle with the tiniest nuance that still has the capacity to manifest discord. Then, of course, there's the steep and swift descent into the realms of verbal abuse if you really want to spiral out of control with your communication and create serious damage.

Here's a list of ways that people can often personally attack that is abusive and limiting.

Please hold compassion for yourself if you have ever blurted any of these statements out of your mouth (or said them to yourself). The intention here is to shine a light on the toxic insults and take the option to speak so violently off the table. Remember: feel, heal, reveal. Here it goes:

You're weak.
You're fat.
You're pathetic.
You're scrawny.
You're a bitch.
You're a fool.
You're a bastard.
You're so stupid.

And then there're the threats, that are either half-full or half-empty. When we threaten like this, it's like flexing a toxic need for control over the situation.

I'm leaving.
I want a divorce.
I'm out of here.
I can't take this anymore.
If you don't change, I swear to God, I will . . .

Remember, you have the power to write the path forward (or backward) for your relationship, whether it's with your spouse, your lover, friends, family, or even coworkers. And here're a few examples of how we place universals and absolutes into the mix of conflict.

You NEVER listen to me!
You're ALWAYS complaining.
You behave like this EVERY time.

When you hurl absolutes at a person, you limit them and you don't allow for the safe space to have a conscious conversation. I've done it so many times that the undoing and unlearning has been quite a journey. I still slip up from time to time when I am emotionally depleted, but I always remember the power I have to create healing, unity, oneness, and togetherness with my choice of words. Here are words you need to say a lot more, especially to the people you love and to remind yourself how to Be the Love.

I love you.
I'm grateful for you.
I appreciate you.
Thank you.
I see you.

The two most transformative words you will ever say and need to learn how to say in a relationship with other humans are these: *I'm sorry.* And I'm not talking about a shallow, hollow, people-pleasing, empty apology. I'm talking about a full-bodied, emptied-out, humble, and sincere apology from the core of your heart. The ability to genuinely apologize and take responsibility for your part in any kind of disagreement is a spiritual rite of passage. When you can get out of the need and addiction to being right and can meet someone in the middle with such a deep sense of self-responsibility, then ultimately you are winning at the game of life. So how can you better stand guard at the doorway to your own thoughts and feelings? The answer is simple—use affirmations.

THE POWER OF AFFIRMATIONS IN ACTION

Throughout this book, we have been introduced to various new affirmations, but I want to share a more in-depth look at them in relation to personal growth.

We all have emotional wounds or issues that need a little more love and attention in order to heal.

Affirmations are not magic beans, Band-Aid solutions, or a clever way to trick the Universe into thinking that you have your shit together when clearly you don't (at present). Affirmations will not work unless you are willing to dive into the emotional work that needs to be done and be truly honest about where you are. You breathe in the good and exhale the less than desirable.

Words that inspire, empower, and excite you have the power to override the current programming you have in your mind and help to form new beliefs, which in turn will help to shift the landscape of your current reality. It's also an incredible access point to the power of the present moment.

But what if you're sending out the wrong message that will backfire in your attempts to create empowering change in your life? What if your "affirmations" are actually sabotaging your results? In fact, there is one affirmation I've seen people sharing regularly on social media that you should definitely replace if you use. The most alarming thing is that the people that post this share it with such beautiful confidence and excitement. I literally cringe every time I read or see it. And that is . . .

I AM NOW DEBT-FREE!

If you're up to your eyeballs in debt, this affirmation sends out the call to attract more debt. The word *debt* is a tough one to override with your feelings, so the Universe still hears the word *debt* followed by the vibrational command of "Bring me more!" The word *free* is another interesting element to examine because it neutralizes the command too. So the words *debt* and *free* actually cancel one another out.

Instead, an effective reframe would be:

I AM NOW LIVING IN ABUNDANCE!

or

I AM NOW FINANCIALLY FREE!

YOUR WORDS MAGNETIZE
YOUR REALITY

I remember when I was being crushed under the weight of massive credit card debt back in 2009. The banks were calling my phone at least three times a day, and all I could tell them was the same thing:

"I'm sorry, I don't have the money."

I remember going into the bank and arranging a payment plan because I was experiencing such terrible financial hardship. My chosen affirmation at the time was . . . you guessed it . . .

"I AM NOW DEBT-FREE!"

Debt, debt, debt.

When I made the switch in my mind and my heart to use the power word of *abundance*, the prosperity started to trickle into my reality, slowly but surely. It was actually somewhat of a two-part process. I removed words of lack and didn't share my struggles verbally with others.

What I mean by this is that the more you focus your energy on a topic, the more that topic will reinforce itself into your reality. I had to get really good at distracting myself when I felt the thoughts sliding into the abyss of limited thinking. I would turn my attention to watching TV shows that had great levels of abundance in them like home renovation shows and movies about rich people. I would mentally send blessings to people who drove expensive cars. I was tuning in my awareness on every level to align with prosperity. I also set the powerful intention to be very supportive and vocal about the success of others on social media. If someone was celebrating a milestone, I was genuinely happy to congratulate them.

HOW TO SET POWERFUL INTENTIONS WITH CLARITY

Setting intentions is your own beautiful and intimate ritual—it's the conversation that you're initiating with the Universe that says:

"Listen up, cosmic entities: I AM READY TO STEP INTO ACTION!"

Intention setting is the first step in the manifesting process and changing your life to be the love that you wish to feel. It is the kick-starting spark and creative power that pushes our desires to be heard by the Universe so the law of attraction can work her magic.

There are three very important elements that must be considered when you're about to embark on the delicious journey inward to set intentions from your heart to manifest.

They are *clarity*, *specificity*, and *energetic action*.

1. **Clarity:** To gain clarity about what you really want to manifest in your life, you'll need to dive in deep and ask yourself some powerful questions. Getting clear about *why* you want things is crucial. For instance, if you intend to manifest a luxury car like a Rolls Royce so that you can drive to your ex's house and show him how hot and rich you are, then you're not dreaming up a better life for yourself from a place of balance. Obviously, it's coming from a place of spite and shallowness—which is a call from your soul to heal that pain.

2. When you speak your intentions into existence, it's all about homing in on the areas of your life that need more illumination. Get clear about how you want to feel more than the "stuff." This means that when material things make your intention-setting list, you can *feel* good about it without just focusing on the material side of things.

3. **Specificity:** When setting your intentions, you must remember that the Universe loves, adores, and thrives on specificity when it comes to your modes of communication. When you're not clear and concise about the specific details of what you wish to manifest, then you leave yourself open to manifesting by default. Believe it or not, but most people do it this way! They say phrases like "I don't know" or "I'm not sure" when asked what they want.

4. One example is that if you set the intention to just "lose weight," you could be asking for a tummy bug that would make you sick enough to lose weight fast through having explosive diarrhea, or worse yet, you could lose an arm or a leg! Now I know this sounds morbid, but rotten things can happen to people who don't dive into the beautiful details and design their life the way they really want to.

5. I once set the intention to receive a gift from the Universe within twenty-four hours. I didn't say what I would like or enjoy, I just stated *gift* without specific details. Within about eighteen hours, a random man on Facebook messaged me an up-close and personal photo of his penis. What was really funny is the fact that he told me it was a "gift" from him to me. No, thanks, buddy. See? Be specific.

6. **Energetic Action:** I have thousands of manifesting students all around the world, and the one thing that always makes me laugh is how people don't anticipate that there is really exciting work to conduct when you wake up and consciously start creating the life of your dreams. Your role is to remove any energetic blocks that are getting in your way. This could be in the form of removing toxic relationships from your life, you could examine your language patterns, you could start to look after your body in a whole new way. The idea is that you are changing

your vibration through being aware of how to manage your energy toward your desired outcome. The bottom line is that you must take energetic action and use your voice to create change.

WHAT I WISH FOR YOU, I WISH FOR MYSELF

The ability to celebrate the success of others is actually one of the most powerful tools in your spiritual toolbox, especially if you congratulate someone verbally. It's a reminder that the energy you put out there will always return to you.

But would you call yourself a jealous person in any way? Are you able to truly feel and celebrate the success of others? Or are you always making it all about yourself and feel like something is rightfully yours before anyone else can experience it? But what if you can't feel happy when others are happy? For many, the green-eyed monster of envy is a powerful adversary.

Seeing other people who have effortlessly managed to manifest their desires can be a huge emotional trigger and reason for upset and distress. I remember the time following my miscarriages when I would all of a sudden see pregnant people everywhere or friends would be announcing that they were expecting. I even had people that would hide their happy news from me because they didn't want to upset me since I was having such a tough time emotionally. I think it all boils down to grace and being aware enough to not take everything so personally.

At Christmastime a few years ago, I was shopping in Whole Foods in Las Vegas, and I heard two elderly ladies conversing and then ending their interaction. One of the women said, "I wish for you what I wish for myself." She reached out and held both of the other lady's hands, and there was a lovely energetic exchange of consciousness.

I thought this was incredibly beautiful; it was like a gracious twist on the old "do unto others" quote from the Bible. This phrase also spoke very deep volumes about what it actually requires to raise your vibration and *be* the essence of that which you desire. This practice is not for the fainthearted because it can be extremely confronting for sure. Sometimes it's hard to extend kindness when you feel like your prayers have gone unanswered by the Universe.

I'll give you a real-life example of being mean-spirited. Sean is the CEO of our company, Soul Space Media. He is such an incredible leader of our team and our company culture, and he ensures that our business runs smoothly. In 2017, he was invited to speak onstage in front of three thousand people at one of the largest conventions on the topic of digital marketing. He was going to use the SarahProut .com brand as a case study. In just a few days, he had prepared a keynote, even though he hadn't had any professional speaker training. He bought a sharp, tailored Ted Baker suit, and as soon as he was onstage, he looked like a million bucks. He crushed his presentation, and when I was watching him address the crowd, I have never been prouder. He was amazing—charismatic, likable, knowledgeable, and hot. I told him he was good, but secretly, I was threatened by how good he was. I didn't have the confidence to stand onstage at that point and speak effectively, so I was mean-spirited. However, this experience gave me the beautiful opportunity to ask myself some questions about how I could claim my own power in that way.

Just two years later, Sean had his own funky feelings of wanting to speak again when it was my turn to take the stage in Bali. It felt like we had to get really good at allowing each other the space we needed to shine and to thrive. It's ultimately a space of cocreating.

When we got married in 2013, our first dance wedding song was "Mirrors" by Justin Timberlake. Some of the lyrics of the song include:

It's like you're my mirror
My mirror staring back at me
I couldn't get any bigger
With anyone else beside of me

These evocative lyrics spoke to me as we definitely have been each other's mirrors over the years. When we can truly get into a space of support for the people we love in our life and ditch our own unclaimed, disowned parts of ourselves that get boosted by ego, then we can be the love we desire to experience. Part of moving into this new phase of awareness in your life is to examine the people that you surround yourself with. How will they impact your life in the future? The fastest way to tell if someone in your life is toxic is how they are able to celebrate the joy in your life without making it about themselves. Of course, in any friendship or relationship, you should construct a mutually beneficial support system where there is a lot of give and a lot of take, but not just take, take, take. Sometimes you can even have people in your life who want to sabotage your success because they don't feel very good about themselves. These people will poop on your parade like nobody's business. Sometimes it's so subtle you don't even know that they are slowly chiseling away at your sense of self.

When you get out of your own head and you give from a place of not expecting anything in return, then you will experience emotional freedom. It will distract you from suffering or anything crappy happening in your life right now and give you an opportunity to lead from your soul. The good news is that life is cyclic, and that as time progresses, you will heal your wounds or perceived difficulties and turn them into wisdom.

SPEAKING UP AND YOUR THROAT CHAKRA

In chapter 3, I mentioned that on the day where I was speaking onstage in Bali for the first time, I developed a sore throat. I believe that this manifested because I wasn't yet truly grounded in my personal power. Yes, I could tell my story with conviction, but I still didn't feel like I had the clarity and the healing I needed to be truly comfortable being so visible. Only a few months earlier, I did two rounds of an incredible speakers' boot camp. I invested in this powerful training because I wanted to hone my skills as a speaker on a stage. I wanted to be more confident with my message and how I delivered it.

Before we began the boot camp, the trainers emailed us a script to memorize that we would deliver in front of the other seminar attendees. The time came for me to deliver the rehearsed script, and the way it worked was that we had to deliver the piece of content until everyone in the room agreed in unison that we'd nailed it. What constituted completion was tone, body language, confidence, eye contact, and use of the space on the stage. It took me over forty times to get it right. In the beginning, I truly believed that I was speaking loudly. Now I'm a fairly soft-spoken person, but I don't think I really knew at that point how to embrace my power and use my voice to its full projected capacity.

There are seven energy centers, or chakras, in the body, and my throat chakra must have been about as blocked as a toilet with severe plumbing issues. Here's a list of the emotional signs that you might have a blocked throat chakra, which can stop you from using your word as your wand:

- Fear of speaking
- Inability to express thoughts
- Shyness
- Inconsistency in speech and actions
- Social anxiety

I had all these symptoms and realized that I had the voice of a girl and not of a woman. It was time for me to step into the ownership of my power. If words and the words we choose to use hold such tremendous transformational energy, then the way we use them (the tone, the pitch, the volume) must be a vital part of the process. When I learned how to fully embrace the power of my voice, my words, and being more intentional with my communication skills, my entire world began to change.

Within just a few months of my newfound skill, I was offered two highly lucrative speaking gigs in New York and New Jersey.

SPEAKING TO HEAL PHYSICAL WOUNDS

Every year on New Year's Eve, I have an intention-setting ritual when I write down all my goals, dreams, wishes, and desires for the coming year. I reflect with gratitude for the year that is ending and then turn my attention to what I am excited to create and attract next. It was only two years earlier that I'd written the intention: "I will manifest a speaking gig at the same event as Tony Robbins." Keep in mind that I was still super shy and timid, and I set this intention way out of my comfort zone. After all, Tony Robbins is one of the biggest and most well-known names in the personal development industry. I had no idea who I had to become to be sharing a stage at an event like that. And in 2019, the invitation arrived and required me to prepare my keynote. I would be speaking at the same event as Tony Robbins, Pitbull, and many other well-known industry leading experts. I was to get paid more than I used to make in a year for just forty-five minutes of my time on a stage.

Remember when I said that my stomach was a shame that I would carry with me, and tuck into my pants, for nearly eighteen years? Well, I did, and for the last few years I felt okay with that—I was okay with the wrinkles and the beautiful stretch marks. I had made total peace with my body, and so it was more about feeling strong in my body that I was seeking to experience. When I was onstage in Bali, I could feel my core stomach muscles felt weak, and I experienced back pain from being in high heels for so long. It felt like there was a weak spot in my abdomen that was stopping me from using my voice to its full capacity.

Oddly enough, when I was questioning my core strength, I got contacted and approached by the producer of a reality TV show. The show concept was all about radical transformations. They would pay for my operation here in America (I think it was in Florida), and they would film the entire process. I really tried on that concept and asked myself if it was something that I'd be willing to do. I'd shut down the option in my mind of ever having a tummy tuck, and yet it was coming to my doorstep for free! And then I thought of the implications. Would I really want the world seeing me have a catheter bag that needed to be emptied?

Or did I want people to see me like on those medical shows like *Botched,* where I would be unconscious on an operating table? I just didn't want to do that. So I politely declined.

However, I couldn't shake the feeling of wondering what it would be like to have a flat stomach. What if I could wear a bikini again? And what if I didn't even have to think about my stomach ever again? Side note here: you don't have to have a flat stomach to wear a bikini. The point is that I was tired of wondering what it would be like to have a stomach that felt stronger. I had the money to make the decision, but I felt selfish making that time for myself to invest in the transformation.

The first step was to get curious and get some questions answered, so I booked a consultation with a plastic surgeon in Las Vegas. After this session, I made the empowered decision to move forward with the tummy tuck. I remember lying on the bed before I was going into the operating theater, and they gave me all my medications and took my blood pressure. I was marked up like an essay paper with black Sharpie marker. I can't look at a Sharpie in the same way again because my doctor marked up all the places where the flesh would be removed from my body. I remember saying goodbye and feeling the sense of how proud of myself I was for making this decision because I felt like I needed to be really brave.

When I woke up, I was so drugged. I don't even really remember getting home. But I do remember that the first couple of days were really, really rough. I had to be on heavy pain meds, and Sean, my amazing husband, was emptying my drains. I mean, this is grisly business. It was disgusting. And I felt like I had been hit by a bus. I had a walking frame, and it took me over ten minutes to walk to somewhere that would normally take me ten seconds. I'm so glad this was not part of a television show, that's for sure.

It was such an incredible journey of mindfulness and remembering to use my communication effectively. I had to remember that my body would take as long as it needed to recover. I had to watch myself go from being so badly bruised and all stitched up to, day by day, getting a bit better and a bit stronger. I kept saying, "I am healed. I am strong. I am powerful."

About a month into my journey, I started using surgical tape to help heal my scar, which ran from one hip to the other. The tape started irritating me, and I started scratching. And this is where it gets a little bit squeamish. What I noticed is that my wound was healing really nicely until it began to open up. I started to panic. Now keep in mind, I had to speak onstage in mid-August. My wound opened up in early August. I'd done all this great healing by using affirmations and using my word as my wand—it was incredible. It was incredible until the wound opened up like something from a horror movie. Three holes appeared on my wound. The largest hole was probably about as big as a tablespoon or a box of matches. Then there were two other smaller holes that looked like flared nostrils, for want of a better analogy. All I knew was that it looked scary. It looked like you could shine your phone flashlight into my abdomen and see my pancreas. It was ghastly, and it looked nightmarish. And I panicked.

There was also an orangey liquid coming out of it, so there was massive risk of infection. To be clear, it wasn't the surgeon's fault. It was my own body's ability to heal. Now, keep in mind that I had a lot of scar tissue from the three C-sections that I'd had. Our bodies react and respond differently, and there's nothing that you can do to predict this will happen.

I used my words to heal my stomach as fast as I could. I used affirmations like:

I am healed.
I will be okay.
I feel stronger every day.

I listened to healing-frequency audios and meditated for hours, clutching different crystals, and I was praying to God as much as I could for a miracle to take place.

I went to my plastic surgeon because it looked so freaky, and I was really frightened that I would perhaps get a bad infection. I just wanted to go to the emergency room and get sewn up. The reality is that when you have a tummy tuck wound opening up, it needs to grow new skin to heal.

"You know what? You just have to wait it out," said my doctor.

"I've got to be on a stage at an event with Tony Robbins in a few weeks! How can I do this?" I pleaded with him.

I had to wear a super-thick maternity pad over my wound because it was leaking so much. The doctor said it was the same hue as Tropicana Punch. Gross.

"The show must go on, and you have to be prepared to do whatever it takes. You will be okay. It looks scary, but it's not scary. You just have to be patient. You have to grow the flesh back so it can seal the wound." My doctor was calm and collected.

I had to learn to trust my body, and my body was doing everything it could to heal. The weeks flew by, and I went to New Jersey to get on this stage at this incredible event. As I went through the airport scanner, the scan detected an anatomical anomaly in my body because I had these pockets of space in my abdomen in which I could probably have smuggled drugs from state to state or country to country if I'd really wanted to. I had to explain to the security staff that I just had an operation and it was not going so well. They carefully patted me down and allowed me to pass.

And so I spoke onstage. It was one of the best and most rewarding events and experiences of my life because I got to talk to people and share my work. The crowd had no idea that I was wearing a pad on an open and leaking wound, and I proved to myself that words have the power to heal, to move us through difficult situations, and our self-talk can either make or break us.

VOWS AND YOUR WORD AS YOUR BOND

Another one of my all-time favorite books is called *The Four Agreements* by Don Miguel Ruiz. The book draws inspiration from a set of spiritual beliefs held by the ancient Toltec people to help readers transform their lives into a new experience of freedom, true happiness, and love. According to Ruiz, everything a person does is based on agreements they have made with themselves, with God (or the Universe), and with others.

Agreement 1 is this: *Be Impeccable with Your Word.*

Ruiz states that while this agreement is the most important, it is the most difficult one to honor.

So here's my question for you. Are you a person who follows through with a promise? Or do you give yourself permission to chicken out, bail out, flip-flop, or be flaky?

To avoid pain and to be a good friend, partner, and good human, you must learn how to do the things you say you are going to do. If you make a promise, keep it. More importantly, if you take an oath or make a vow, keep it. This forges a path of integrity.

Yes, you have the power to change your mind, but only if you have a solid record of being a person that sticks to their word. I am a very punctual person. If I say I'm going to be somewhere at a specific time, I am there or you will know if I'm late before the time I need to be there. If I tell you I'm going to do something, I will do it. Disappointing people is not something I want to do.

And most important is that I honor my own word. If I promise myself something, or make a promise to myself, I will keep it. At the point I am writing this, I can't remember specifically the vows I made to my husband on my wedding day because I modified them slightly. I wrote them on a card somewhere, and I need to find them. This was the draft, though, that I'd emailed myself the day before we exchanged our vows:

Sean, I will love you with all of me, for the rest of my life. I promise to cherish your heart and nurture your dreams, goals, wishes, and desires as

we walk through this life experience hand in hand.
I promise to show up in each and every moment
and enjoy this miraculous journey with you. I am
so deeply honored that you have chosen to spend
your life with me. And I promise, from the bottom
of my heart, that I will always be your best friend,
your biggest fan, your strongest support system,
your lover, your wife, and your home. You have
completed my heart, Sean Patrick Simpson, as
you have shown me that true love really exists and
that anything is possible. You loved me enough to
move across the world, you loved me enough to step
up and make the conscious choice to raise Thomas
and Olivia with me. I'm really looking forward to
growing old with you, raising more babies with you,
and eventually having grandchildren. I'm looking
forward to waking up next to you each morning
and cuddling up to you at the end of each day.

Revisit your promises. Rewrite them. Make these
promises each and every day to make the choice to be
more intentional with your life. I recently wrote this
love note for my Sean:

To my husband,

*I want to BE in love with you. I want to GROW
more and more in love with you. I want to love you*

FOREVER. I will create a future and build a life with you that is magnificent.

Love,
Your Wife. xo

BE MINDFUL AND CELEBRATE THE POWER OF CREATIVE ENERGY

Every word you choose to use, every phrase and every expression, is calling your reality into existence. This is why it's so important to be mindful of the words you choose to speak. Words have the power to harm or to heal, to nourish or to contaminate. And it's your duty of care and honor when you are conversing with other humans to lead by example. This doesn't give you permission to be a pain in the ass about it, though. You can't call other people out on their language patterns, especially if you are still learning how to do it too. The beauty and transformative energy is in awareness of how you can express yourself. Let me ask you this: If you had to create a chart based on your most frequently used words and key phrases, would it be more based on scarcity (not having enough) or abundance (feeling grateful)? If you regularly use words like *hate* or *ugly* or *whatever*, then you are actively limiting your experience of abundance. It's a signal to the Universe in vibration form to say what you are ready to receive.

Your word is your wand, and the more you can become aware of your language patterns, the more you can master your fate intentionally.

Collective Kindness Exercise 6

Tell someone you love them. You can say this to someone you actually love, or you can send the energy of love and appreciation in your mind. Saying, "I LOVE YOU," is beautiful energy to put out into the world. It contributes to the collective energy of being the love.

THINGS THAT MADE ME FEEL MORE INTENTIONAL

1. **I became aware of the power of specificity:** It's truly no wonder that most people feel unheard or misunderstood, especially in relationships. In my business, when I need someone to complete a project for me, I need to be as specific as possible with my requirements to make sure the job gets done. When

I was studying journalism in my twenties, we learned that to craft an effective and informative article, we needed to answer the five Ws and the H—*who, why, where, when, what,* and *how*. It wasn't until my mentor Scott deMoulin introduced me to the concept known as the Precision Model that I began to see how specificity plays a vital role in success. This model is often used to optimize business communication and to extract levels of exactness. To quote Mark Twain, "The difference between the right word and the almost right word is the difference between lightning and a lightning bug."

2. **I committed to being more intentional with my words:** There is no greater way to become more intentional with your words than when you are raising children. Every expression you choose to share with a child helps them to form their beliefs about themselves and the world around them. I became committed to leading by example for my kids and being more mindful of how I express myself in front of them.

3. **I realized that "message sent" does not always mean "message delivered":** A person can nod and smile and say they understand what you're saying or what you've been through, but they might not have the faintest clue! I used to do this in math class when I was a child. I would nod and smile and tell the teacher

that I fully understood how to do an equation, and then I would fail each and every test. Why? Because I would rather fail than look stupid in the moment. It's not exactly a solid strategy.

4. **I experienced how being vulnerable is the key to connection:** One of the ways that our business grew so quickly is that I was willing to share my most personal stories with complete strangers on the internet. Take the Goalcast video, for example—if I hadn't been willing to share my story of surviving domestic violence, then comment threads of others sharing their own stories wouldn't have been possible. You can only do this if you have pure intentions. You don't want to emotionally manipulate others into trusting you; you want to be a safe space and a sacred container for others to feel heard and understood.

5. **I remembered the power of alignment:** You're not meant to get along with every single human being. As the old saying goes, "Birds of a feather flock together." You will be naturally drawn to and aligned with people that are on your wavelength or people that have tremendous gifts of difference to offer you, and you for them. After I separated from my ex and I was out in the dating world, I was trying my best to make matches with people who were clearly not right for me. I had to learn how to trust the power of alignment. If I wanted to truly find a place to belong,

a group of people who inherently understood my soul on a deep level, then I had to trust the Universe had a plan for me. Whatever is meant for you will manifest. Whatever is not in alignment will fall away. It's a pretty cool cosmic system, actually.

JOURNAL PROMPTS: Be the Love and Embrace That Your Word Is Your Wand

FEEL: How have your words contributed to you feeling abundant and empowered in your life? How have your words contributed to painful experiences in your life? How do you feel when you examine the way that you intentionally use communication with yourself and others?

_____

_____

_____

HEAL: What are the ten most empowering words that you could use more on a regular basis? What are words that you will become aware of not to use so much anymore in your everyday vocabulary?

_____

_____

_____

REVEAL: What will you intentionally speak into existence? How can you anchor the awareness and remember to be more mindful about how you choose to use your words?

_____

_____

_____

7

Everything Is Energy

Close your eyes, breathe in deeply, exhale, and then say this affirmation: *I am love.*

Everything is energy, but what we don't often stop to ask is what that energy is made from. It's LOVE. Love is the highest form of pure consciousness, vibration, or energy. That's why there are so many songs written that include the word *love,* or why movies are based around love stories. The Universe, God, Source, or the Force IS the frequency of love. You are love manifested as a human throughout your lifetime and beyond. Love has the power to transcend time and space. It can be shared, sent, experienced, indulged in, but it can never be lost. Love is ever present and always available. Remember that it's there.

There's this feeling that I experience every now and then where I feel so incredibly grounded and connected to pure love. It usually appears at the change of seasons, after having a big cry, or when I recover from feeling unwell. It's usually the breakthrough after the breakdown. I feel at home. I feel at peace and emptied out. I trust that everything is perfect in the way that it is manifesting. This doesn't mean that I know with certainty that everything is going to unfold without pain or struggle, but these momentary feelings are a glimmer and a glimpse of what I call *pure reality*.

Pure reality is when you can be present in who you are and what you are doing at any given moment. This is the gateway to your intuition and being ready to work with the Be the Love philosophy to feel, heal, and reveal. These moments are filtered through being completely accepting of what is. It's the space between right and wrong. It's the magical vortex between what is known and unknown—the free-flowing experience between clarity and cloudiness. It's acceptance of the energetic flow of life and the embodiment of unconditional love.

My grandmother Nana Mollie was a constant source of love in my life.

During her visits to stay with my family in the 1990s, we would often have deep and in-depth discussions about faith and the afterlife. Nana believed in the concept of heaven and said that one day when I crossed over, she would be waiting for me. As she said this, she would hold my hand, and I could feel her promise to facilitate this intention. Mollie's address was 116 Lenton

Street, in New Zealand—I'll get to the reason why this is important in a moment.

New Zealand, early 1999

It all felt so familiar because my mother grew up in this home. We drove down the long gravel driveway, and a small, white-haired woman stood on the back doorstep eager to greet me. Wearing her signature floral dress, brown woolen cardigan, and clip-on pearl earrings the size of giant peppermints, I could see that it was now difficult for her to stand up straight without feeling strained. She wrapped her arms around me, and I noticed that I was now slightly taller than she was. Nana Mollie's embrace always felt like I was home. I hadn't seen her in a few years, and I had no idea at the time that this would be the very last visit. There was the faint scent of her 4711 cologne. Apparently, it's the fragrance of neroli oil produced from the blossom of the bitter orange tree, always my favorite. She kissed my cheek and then immediately wiped away the residue of her oily pink lipstick mixed with my tears.

"This is Jim," I said to Nana, composing myself. I was a little nervous introducing her to my high school boyfriend, but I trusted that he would be polite and well mannered.

"It's nice to meet you, Mrs. Findlay," Jim said.

They shook hands and exchanged pleasantries.

We walked into the house, and it was just as I had remembered, with stacked-up copies of *National Geographic* and a large dining table that could seat at least ten people in the center of the room. Now it was just holding space for the memories of the people that had been born, lived, and died in the home. My grandmother arrived in the world in 1913 and had lived in this house for her entire life. She even raised her five children here too, who had all grown up and moved away to begin their own lives. My mother was her youngest child out of the five and the most rebellious, according to Nana. To illustrate this, I was shown a bucket of mutilated Barbie doll heads from the 1960s that were either melted, shaved, or had safety pins jammed through their scalps. I'm actually not sure why Nana would keep that as part of her archive of memories, but she did. The surrounding walls were plastered in postcards, children's drawings, newspaper clippings, and happy photographs of her many grandchildren.

This old weatherboard house had seven bedrooms all positioned off a long centralized hallway. As an artist, Nana painted beautiful portraits of the Māori indigenous people of New Zealand. The term *Tā moko* is the permanent marking or tattoo as traditionally practiced by Māori people. I remember Nana telling me that getting the lines of the tattoo right on the portrait was her favorite part of the process; she felt a kinship in some way even though there was no DNA connection. Nana's artwork was displayed all over the house, from copies of old masters' paintings to portraits of her grandchildren and family members. I remember when I was very little, it would feel like many different sets of eyes were following me down the hallway when I got up to use the bathroom in the middle of the night.

That evening, Nana escorted Jim and me to our rooms. I was to sleep in my mother's old room, and because Nana had very Catholic values, Jim would sleep across the hall in my deceased grandfather's old room. When you're staying in a big, old house, there are many things that can go bump in the night, leaving you to feel a tad spooked. The wallpaper tended to exhale when there was a large gust of a breeze blowing through. If any place was going to be haunted, it was surely this one. Nana's room was fairly close to mine, and all throughout the night, I could hear the radio blasting, which made it extremely difficult to sleep.

"Why did you keep the radio on all night, Nana?"

"I didn't, dear. You must be mistaken."

There was a slight tone of defensiveness, so I decided to let it be.

As we were having our breakfast, I realized that it wasn't some eerie ghost radio; it was a tool to manage the fear of living alone. She must have used it like a white noise machine to drown out scary sounds. Imagine being a caretaker for the majority of your life—preparing thousands of meals, washing clothes, and still going to church every Sunday. My grandmother lived through wars and birthing children and losing so many loved ones, including babies. The home was the energy of love, memories of love, and embodiment of a lifetime of service and cycles of growth.

Over the years, I would write letters (that she would then tape to the walls) because this was before the time of email. And I would also call her as often as I could, even though the international calls from Australia to New Zealand were costly. Each time, I would tell her that I loved her. It was only a couple of years later that her health declined, and on the wall of her bedroom in the nursing home facility, she had a photo of her very first great-grandchild—my son, Thomas, whom she never got to meet. Nana Mollie died in 2003. She was so loved, and she taught me how to Be the Love. Every now and then, the number 116 appears to me in various situations. I like to see it as a little wave or a nod from Nana from the nonphysical realm that love never dies.

CONTAINERS OF ENERGY, MEMORIES, AND MAGIC MOMENTS

As I said, Nana kept a bucketful of mutilated Barbie doll heads that my mother used to play with when she was a child. I wasn't sure why she kept them, but I can sort of understand in a weird way. The things we spend time with, devote energy to, or cherish in some aspect have a very specific energetic frequency. They can also access the beauty of nostalgic moments that bring the memories to the forefront of our minds.

A few years before I was born (probably around 1976), my dad was calling me into existence by crocheting a blanket. The word *crochet* is derived from the French term meaning "small hook." Different from knitting, crocheting is a series of interlocking loops made from soft, fine yarn. My dad learned how to do this when he was just a boy because he spent a lot of time indoors due to childhood illness. On a trip to London with my mother, Mr. Tony Prout started to outline what would one day be his daughter's most cherished childhood item. Within the first few days of my life, I was wrapped in the blanket, and it felt like being home. I called my blanket "Cuddly," and it went everywhere with me. I carried around Cuddly like the character Linus from *Peanuts* carried around his security blanket. If I went to school or camp, Cuddly came too. In my teenage years, the blanket was loved so much that it started to disintegrate and break off into pieces. When I moved in with my first husband, I kept a small square of Cuddly in my pillowcase. He knew it was there and jokingly said that I could choose either him or choose Cuddly. I would whisper, "Cuddly. Always Cuddly."

After I had Thomas when I was twenty-one, Cuddly was of course long forgotten about. I had a child that now kept his own blanket and special toy. Thomas loved a bear named Humphrey B. Bear, except he insisted that his toy was to be addressed as "Bear Bear." Bear Bear went everywhere with him. On the day Thomas moved out when he was about to turn nineteen years old, I kept such a brave face until I asked where Bear Bear was. I quickly switched topics and stepped out of the room to have a good cry because of the cyclic nature of life. I didn't want Thomas to see me breaking down. I wanted him to see that I trusted he was a capable young man ready to venture off out into the world. However, that silly toy bear was the container for so much love, so much life and change that had unfolded over the last eighteen-plus years. Bear Bear and Thomas were about to leave the nest and not be under the same roof any longer with me. I know it might seem simple, but the energy of these kinds of transitions are what the fabric of life is created from.

And where is Cuddly today, you might ask? Cuddly, or the remnants of Cuddly, are currently in an archival box at my dad's house in Melbourne, Australia.

CREATE LOVING ENERGY WITH SPONTANEOUS ADVENTURES

Before the pandemic began in 2020, I was committed to flying my parents out to spend time with us in

America each year. It's tricky when you have divorced parents, though, because I had to make time for each of them separately. Back in 2019, my dad had some various health issues but was usually more than willing to make the trip from Australia despite how the flight was usually long and uncomfortable for him. In his early seventies, he had pneumonia twice, so breathing was a bit of a task for him. Low oxygen levels sometimes messed with his circulation and made it difficult for him to walk. This was highly unusual for my dad because for most of his life (outside of childhood), he had been very active—mowing lawns, gardening, throwing extravagant art exhibitions, and walking everywhere he went. One evening just before Christmas, Dad was visiting us in Las Vegas. The sun was just about to go down, and the air was frosty and crisp. Many people think it never gets cold in Vegas, but it does. I told Dad I would take him for a drive out into the desert so we could watch the sunset. Just on the outskirts of the town we lived in was a place called Summerlin, near Red Rock Canyon National Conservation Area. Since it wasn't open, I drove down a small dirt road so we could see the red rocks anyway. I parked the car at the base of a hill.

"Let's get out and walk," I said excitedly.

"Oh no, it's too cold. I could die, Sarah!"

It was such a beautiful evening. The dusky sky was pink and orange, and I knew the view would be exquisite from higher up the hill. I was determined to create a special memory with my dad while he was with me in Las Vegas.

"Well, if you're going to die, up that hill is a nice place to make your exit, don't you think?" We always joked about stuff like this, so he knew I was prompting him to accept the challenge.

Dad agreed, and we slowly started to climb the small hill, one foot in front of the other, which must have felt like climbing the Himalayas for him at that time.

"Oh, it's magnificent!" He was grounded in a present state of awe.

I could see him absorbing the beauty of the Nevada desert, the divine hue of the clouds, and the joy of climbing a small hill he didn't think he could climb. It was like being in one of his watercolor paintings. It felt like a magical moment, just me and my dad. It almost felt otherworldly. My face felt frozen, but we stood in deep reverence from the experience and then walked back to the car. Thankfully, my car had butt warmers; the icy air had numbed my caboose. The point here is that if you want to switch up the energy and activate memories of love, then you need to venture out of your comfort zone just like I shared with you in chapter 3. In this particular experience, my dad could have chosen to stay afraid, to not fly across the world to visit us in America, or to not climb up that hill. But he did.

That's an act of moving toward oneness rather than staying separate because of being afraid. It's a memory that I will love and cherish forever. It's so exciting to do things you wouldn't normally do.

I've mentioned that throughout life we have two choices in each moment—we can move in the direction of fear or in the direction of love. We can also move toward oneness, or we can move away through the process of separation. When we choose togetherness and oneness, then we have the power to heal the collective energy of humanity.

BLESSINGS IN THE LESSON OR (HOPEFULLY) THE ENERGY YOU PUT OUT THERE WILL RETURN

It was a Saturday morning in Las Vegas. My family and I decided to venture into town to have breakfast at the Cosmopolitan. After our meal, we went for a walk. It was crowded and slightly chaotic. Tourists, shoppers, and sightseers were all swarming around us. As we crossed the bridge from the Cosmopolitan to the Aria Resort and Casino, we were approached by what appeared to be a Buddhist monk. He had a shaved head and was wearing monk-like attire—long saffron robes and bare feet.

He was holding a book, and he was collecting donations for a temple. The book had many different names and the amounts donated by each person.

He handed me a golden card that read *Work Smoothly, Lifetime Peace*. The man had very broken English. Before any money was handed over, he placed prayer beads around my wrist. I looked to Sean to give a small donation. All he had was a hundred-dollar bill. "This is your lucky day!" Sean said as he handed over the cash.

Oh, my bighearted husband! My heart always melts at his generosity. The monk then placed a string of mala beads around Lulu's neck (she was three at the time), one around mine, and then one around Sean's. Sean wrote down in the book the donation of one hundred dollars—even though I already did that and the monk started to aggressively gesture for a second hundred dollars because it was listed.

Sean explained the donation was from both of us and he would correct it with the pen, and the monk started to appear agitated. At first, he was grateful, and then when he realized there was no more money, his hand gestures became super weird and aggressive.

We walked away quickly to get to our next location. We didn't speak. After about five minutes, I told Sean that the mala beads felt weird. My intuition was telling me to take them off. They didn't feel right. Even Lulu was willing to part with them because she sensed they felt funky. Sometimes I get strange vibes from things, and the mala necklace was giving me the creeps.

"You know, Sean, I think that was some kind of scam," I said.

Sure enough, a quick online search revealed that the panhandling, hustling monk scam was a thing. It's not just in Vegas but in many cities around the world.

"He needs the money more than I do," Sean said.

I felt a little mad at first and then decided to let it go. After all, nothing that is truly yours can ever be lost. I teach this to my manifesting students, so it was an opportunity to walk the talk. Here's what we actually received for handing over the hundred dollars:

- Strengthened intuition to feel the energy of a situation
- A reminder to pay attention to our environment and not get swept up with the hustle and bustle of others around us
- A reminder to always ask what the money is intended for
- A reminder to not be so naive to believe that someone dressed in spiritual attire is actually spiritual

When we pondered this interaction, we realized it was a valuable lesson in awareness and energy management. This was worth way more than just a hundred dollars. In fact, this lesson could have saved us thousands of dollars.

Sometimes you might not know what you want until you can picture it. Let's take the idea of buying a new dress, for example. You see that it looks great on the hanger or on the photo of it in the online store. You might buy it before trying it on, only to discover that it doesn't quite fit right when you wear it. The same is for your goals, intentions, and how you perceive experiences.

GUIDING YOUR ENERGY WITH LOVING VISUALIZATION

The art of visualization is one of the most powerful tools that you can utilize. There are so many resources out there about the art of visualization, so it can feel a little difficult to know where to begin. Visualization is used in many different ways, whether it's high-performance athletes who like to visualize the outcome of a race or a poker player anticipating the moves of a game. Studies show there are numerous great benefits to picturing the outcome in your mind first. I believe this is why there are so many people who work in the space of peak performance (hypnotherapists, for example) who help to support people so they can perform at their best. If you are in this game of life, you need to get really good at how to play it.

So where do you start? I have been practicing the art of creative visualization for at least thirty years. I was around ten years old when I started. I would visualize what it would be like to spend time with the boy that I had a crush on. I would picture myself sitting under a tree with beautiful pink cherry blossoms covering its branches. I would visualize myself wearing a long, flowy purple gown. I don't know where that idea came from, but it was almost the same color as the cover of my *Dear Universe* book.

As I would visualize, I would feel calm and peaceful, and it was like a utopian experience. Imaginative daydreaming is a really interesting and powerful tool to engage in. And the great thing about remembering your powers of visualization is that you can start to do that now, whether you are wanting to attract true love, whether you are wanting to attract abundance. You have that ability within you to know what ultimately will serve you the most.

When I was fourteen, I loved drawing so much. I would create bright and vibrant designs that looked like colorful wallpaper from the 1960s. I mostly drew what I called *cosmic flowers*, and they had a very definite style to them. On a long school vacation, I decided to send my designs to the top greeting card and wrapping paper manufacturers to see if they'd be interested in printing my work. This was in the days before the internet, so I photocopied my designs at the school library, typed out a cover letter on a typewriter, and found the corporate headquarters to mail them to by simply looking in the phone book.

Weeks passed, and I didn't hear anything back. During this time, I visualized what it would feel like to see my wrapping paper designs on the shelves of the top department stores around the world and with the paper having my name stamped on it. Every night before bed, I could see in my mind's eye the colorful displays of my work and how great it felt to know I had created something from just a tiny idea. Sure enough, I got a call from an executive at Hallmark, the largest greeting card manufacturer in the world, to come in for a meeting. I had to tell her that I was fourteen, which further intrigued her, and my dad had to drive me to the meeting. Not long after the meeting, I was commissioned a few thousand dollars for my first four designs to be placed in all major department stores in Australia and New Zealand. This was one of my first real tastes of how manifesting actually works. This level of creative empowerment should have placed me on a path to success, but instead, I was still headed for a detour of seeking approval from other people.

When I was nineteen years old, I dropped out of college, much to my parents' disappointment. I had found myself in a very exclusive graphic design program at my chosen school, but it didn't interest me. And I think there were only about a hundred positions available to get into this course. On the day it began, I showed up there and I just didn't feel like it was for me. So I decided to take a break, and I didn't actually know if I'd end up going back. During this time, I found myself working in various jobs. I worked in a picture frame factory for a little while doing visual display merchandising and framing people's art prints. And then I landed a job at a lingerie store. It was called Audacity, and it sold high-end lingerie.

Working in this store was a really interesting experience. I didn't wear any of the products sold there, because I couldn't afford them on my tiny weekly wages. We tended to get some interesting characters in the store on a regular basis.

It was during this time that I worked over the road from a picture framing gallery, and this was not the one I've just mentioned; this was at a competing picture framing gallery. I was really into a guy who worked there. I would watch him from a distance and wonder who he was. He was tall and wore a leather jacket and had a long brown ponytail that could have easily been a man bun before they were fashionable.

I was visualizing what it would be like to connect with this guy. I could sense his energy, so when I was standing in the lingerie store waiting for clients to come in, I would look out over the road and I'd just be able to see what he was doing, and he could see what I was doing as well. And I would visualize in my mind's eye that somehow, our paths would eventually cross.

It wasn't like I was going to go over there and introduce myself, but I would visualize that one day our paths would cross and we would ultimately fall in love and it would be a happily-ever-after story. This guy was really good looking. And so at nighttime, five minutes before I would fall asleep, I would visualize that I was in the art gallery over the road and we could connect on a really deep level. I intentionally placed my thoughts and focus to be in the art gallery, because if he was in the lingerie store, it meant that he was probably shopping for somebody else. During this time, I was still processing grief because I had been dumped by my high school boyfriend, Jim. My heart was broken. He'd paid for the trip to take me to New Zealand to visit Nana Mollie, and now he didn't want to be with me.

Being single as a young adult was something that I wasn't really used to. It felt exciting, but at the same time, it was really scary. And so I would keep visualizing that maybe I would cross paths with the guy who worked in the frame gallery and he would ask me for my phone number. And then one day, I had the inspired idea, and I said to myself, "Okay, Sarah Prout, stop being so silly, stop waiting for things to happen, and take inspired action. It's time to take control of this situation."

He worked in a frame gallery; I was somewhat of an artist, so I thought it would be a genius idea if I could get something framed! I knew this would be an ideal way to move the energy forward. I worked all weekend on a floral piece that would be quite impressive, very highly detailed. On Monday morning before my shift started, I went over there and said, "Hey, I'm Sarah. I work in the lingerie store over the road. Can I get this framed, please?"

And sure enough, he asked me for my phone number because he took the order. So there was number one, my manifestation to exchange numbers. Number two was that we had the potential to get along as friends. There wasn't instant chemistry like I'd thought there might be, and the distant attraction fizzled out within minutes. A surprising turn of events was that he then offered me a job, which I had no idea was going to manifest. It was a Sunday job where I would work in the gallery from midday to 4:00 p.m., and I would take the framing orders or deliver the ones that had already been ordered. They also had artwork on the walls, so I would take sales on behalf of the artists for the artwork. So all this precious time that I had spent visualizing, meeting, and crossing paths with this handsome guy in this gallery space had all converged to this precise point in time.

It was only about a couple of months later on one of my Sunday shifts in the gallery that a guy walked in who just so happened to be my first husband. And so you never know how you are *energetically* charging the space that you visualize in your mind's eye. Now, if I had my time over again, of course I wouldn't change anything even if I could. But for the sake of giving visualization advice, what I could have done differently is that I would have focused on how I *felt* rather than making sure that the location was in the gallery instead of the lingerie store. I wasn't visualizing:

- I feel so cherished.
- I feel so loved.
- I am an empowered woman.
- I feel so seen by the man of my dreams.

That wasn't it. It was the fact that our paths crossed, and that was all I was focusing on. So if you want to attract true love in this most sacred visualization space, tune in to how you feel when you are with this person. Also, and this is a very powerful manifesting tip, focus on them. Not on you, not on how they make you feel, not on what you get out of the relationship—focus on what you give to the relationship, focus on their feelings as well and how you can honor that union.

What kind of a flutter do you place in their heart? It is really important that you flip the script on it, because if you are single right now reading this, there is a person out there who is waiting to manifest you. So switch it up a little bit. And if you are in a relationship that is struggling or you wish there were a deeper level of connection, you can visualize what it's going to take to amplify that level of connection that you have in your current relationship, because relationships ebb and flow. Sometimes they're really hot, heavy, and steamy, and then other times, it's like, *Oh my God, can't you just remember to put the damn toilet seat down, please? Or will you trim your nose and ear hairs?* You're in a phase either of remembering or forgetting.

And as you remember the power you have in your mind's eye, that what you see in your mind you can create and attract, please get very selective about what you allow into this chamber in your mind palace. Get very curious about what you are allowing, what you are programming your mind with, who you are allowing into your life. What kind of energy patterns do you need to set some very strong and self-compassionate boundaries around? And then you can visualize not from a space of limitation or from desperation or from timidness like I was when I was looking to connect with that guy that worked in the frame factory all those years ago. Just remember the power you have to guide your energy. And when you do that, when you get clear about what's inside the walls of your mind, what you are projecting out into the world, you'll be amazed at what begins to come back to you.

A TRUE EXPERIENCE THAT EVERY-THING IS ENERGY

March 23, 2015

Today was the day I would meet my baby. It was 5:00 a.m., and my beloved Sean pulled the car over to the side of the road for us to watch the sunrise together. The breeze from the ocean waves was refreshing and helped me to somewhat ease my nerves. I'd already had a C-section when I gave birth to Olivia nine years earlier, but after the traumatic journey of five miscarriages in a row, I couldn't believe that today was the actual day to finally hold Lulu Dawn in my arms. She would be safe, sound, and earth-side. I felt like I could breathe deeply for once and ease myself into this new chapter of my life.

I had been pregnant for a total of over eighteen months, spanning six pregnancies, to get to this very day, which, interestingly enough, is nearly as long as the gestation period to birth a baby elephant! As the sun rose, we drove into the Noosa Hinterland to make our way to the hospital for the scheduled appointment. Sean and I were eagerly scanning the skies for a rainbow. Every single important moment in our lives together thus far seemed to be punctuated by the presence of a rainbow. However, on this day, it wasn't. This is a powerful reminder of how signs need to naturally find you, instead of you forcing this issue with the cosmos to deliver. For many months, I'd been looking up at the clock to see the time 7:11 displayed, and I couldn't figure out why. I thought that perhaps Lulu could be born weighing seven pounds and eleven ounces, which was a pretty solid bet. I used this occurrence as a sign from the Universe that each day was edging me closer to her safe arrival. It was always a divine reminder.

Earlier in the pregnancy, at just five weeks and three days along, I saw Lulu's heart beating in my belly for the first time. I was bleeding and believed that this pregnancy would end in another miscarriage, so I headed off to the local emergency room to brace myself for the inevitable bad news. After my history of losses, the doctor told me there was just a 20 percent chance that the baby I was carrying would survive. The term he used was *subchorionic hematoma*, which meant that, due to my history, this situation would probably end in loss because blood was pooling around the placenta. Around 1 percent of all pregnancies have a subchorionic bleed. During this time of recurrent loss, I decided to get really good at celebrating milestones. Every day that Lulu's tiny heart was still beating was a cause for celebration. However, the day she was born went radically different from how I had hoped.

The public health system in Australia meant that they had a list of birthing times scheduled for the women booked in for elective C-sections. I was last on the daily list of people to be seen. I was hunched over a pillow, and the anesthesiologist couldn't quite get the needle into my spine in the right place for the epidural to work. After numerous attempts, I was feeling extremely sore and anxious. They found a space that worked quite high up on my spine, and all of a sudden, I lost all feeling below my waist. This is totally normal and to be expected when you have a cesarean section.

I was then wheeled into the operating room, where I was met by Sean. He was so excited and nervous to meet his child for the first time. It took a little while for them to open me up, with lots of weird tugging, pulling, and suction noises, and then the sweet sound of Lulu's cries filled the operating theater! She was safe, sound, and earth-side.

They placed the infant on my chest for a cuddle and to say hello. Her head was covered in hair and was perfect in every way. Sean was then asked to go with the nurse to get Lulu weighed and measured, which is when I was getting stitched up. I started to slowly feel the endorphins leaving from the happy energy of meeting Lulu. In fact, I began to become aware that the anesthetic was starting to wear off too. My body began shaking, and I could feel the air on my open abdomen. It was agony.

The surgeon took a metal tool and asked me if I could feel it pressing into my skin in various places.

"I can feel that! I can feel that!" I said, beginning to hyperventilate. I felt like I could feel warm blood pumping out and leaving my body. It was like some extremely disturbing scene from a horror movie, where the pain was so bad that I thought I was going to die.

The nurses cued in on the situation and rushed Sean and Lulu out of the operating theater. At that point, I started screaming and shaking uncontrollably before they told me that they were putting me to sleep. I was so scared because I didn't know if I was going to wake up or if I would ever get to hold my baby again.

The last thing I remember was passing out but being aware that I was still present in the room outside of myself, if that makes sense. I was hovering above and outside of my body. At that point, the pain had left me and I was aware of being in a holding space and not feeling like I was asleep but being aware that I was somewhere else, up high, above everything and part of everything. Almost like on another level of the hospital where I could see all of the things going on at once.

Then the pain left me. I could see the color pink everywhere and a vibrant selection of colors such as violet, magenta, and the brightest of orange. They looked like the colors of the chakra energy centers. I was in a large corridor that had rooms and doors, just like the hospital, but different. Behind each door, I could simultaneously see different scenes. I could see and feel

Sean sitting with Lulu, I could see my body being stitched up, I could see the nurses, I could see Thomas and Olivia laughing and having fun with my mother, who was looking after them. I felt as if I were one with Lulu and I was peering out into the world from her new perspective. I could see everything that I love aesthetically and admire, such as ornate mirrors, vibrant orchids, purple velvet furniture, large amethyst crystals, and the list goes on. It was like I was flying around this corridor, this weird realm, and not sure how to get back to myself, to my consciousness. I felt infinite and part of the energy of true oneness.

Suddenly, I realized I had no control over waking up, and it became a little scary. I loved this place I was in; it felt peaceful. But the more at peace I felt, the more the memory of who I was and what my purpose was started to fade.

I distinctly remember asking myself, *Am I dead? Who am I?*

I didn't remember who I was. Then I heard a voice say very clearly the names of my children and my love: Thomas, Olivia, Lulu, and Sean. The voice wasn't mine, and it wasn't clear. It was like an anchor of love to return me to who I was. At 7:11 p.m., I woke up back in my body after a thrilling adventure into the infinite.

The nurse said to me, after looking at my hospital wristband, "Welcome back. I have a daughter named

Sarah too, and you share the same birthday. That's weird."

What I gathered from this experience is that we live in a world of infinite possibilities, and the world beyond is the purest essence of infinite unconditional love. We are so much more than our physical reality, and we are spiritual beings in the playground of life.

THE COLLECTIVE INTENTION

Do not feel lonely, the entire universe is inside of you.
—Rumi

As humans, we are connected with intertwining vibrations and energy patterns all mingled together to move through life. However, it's so easy to fall into the trap of forgetting the bigger picture at play. We are sovereign beings, always at a point of choice. We so often get swept up in the humdrum experiences of daily life, such as paying bills, caring for others, or thinking about what to have for dinner. Then there's the ways in which we hand our power over and believe that finding love is something that happens outside of ourselves. But when you become devoted to Being the Love, then you need to remember to pause and to see the love too in every situation. This is especially powerful in challenging times and difficult situations. This means remembering the energy that animates all that exists in this world. It's the truest and purest form of unconditional love. This is the nature of superconsciousness and divine essence. Even if you pause for just a minute a day to sit in stillness and reverence for the energy that keeps the water in the ocean and the stars in the sky, then you connect to the core nature of who you truly are. You are a sovereign spiritual being constructed of pure love.

BEING THE LOVE IS JUST REMEMBERING WHO YOU ARE

Make it your mission to connect with others and do something kind on a daily basis. It could be that you share a link to a cause you are passionate about supporting on social media. It could be that you pay for someone else's coffee behind you in the line at a café. The Universe will often present you with beautiful opportunities to be kind, and you need to be willing to accept the mission. Kindness opens up your heart, it heals the hearts of others, and it's the true embodiment of being the love you wish and intend to feel.

I'll leave you with this . . .

In the great lyrical genius of John Lennon and Paul McCartney:

All you need is love.
So be it and so it is.

Collective Kindness Exercise 7

When you meditate, devote two to three minutes to sending the healing energy of pure LOVE from your heart to the people of this planet, to the planet itself, and to the Universe. This ripples out into the world in the most miraculous of ways to Be the Love.

THINGS THAT MADE ME FEEL LOVED

1. **I allowed myself to receive love:** When you have been hurt, it is so easy to build walls around your heart and never let anyone get close to you. It's the mind's natural defense mechanism that gives the false illusion of being protected from harm. The only way for my relationship with Sean to survive was to let him get close. I had to allow him the space to express love, and I had to receive it instead of rejecting it. For the first few years, if his attempts to love me were letters, they would have been always stamped

with "return to sender." I was healing and didn't feel "perfect" or "worthy enough" to receive love in case it wounded my soul yet again. I didn't believe that my mental health could suffer from the loss. But it was a mutually conflicting situation due to the fact that if I didn't love me, then he couldn't love me. Every loving act, no matter how small, was deeply appreciated because he was willing to see beyond my walls. The key is to allow people to get close to you and trust that their intentions are not to rip your heart out of your chest and turn you into a piñata. I trained myself to feel grateful for acts of love instead of rejecting them. It took time, but the intention to heal illuminated a new path.

2. **I prioritized my relationship with a higher power:** I have mentioned many times before how important it is to connect with the Universe. This can be done either through prayer or through the power of meditation. When I truly started to open my heart up to loving myself unconditionally, I knew that I wasn't doing it alone; I had the support, guidance, wisdom, and compassion of the Universe on my side and in my corner. This meant that every single time I experienced joy or happiness (or any emotion under the sun), I knew it was divine guidance and divine timing in direct relation to the prioritization of my connection with a higher power. Each and every day is a blessing. In fact,

each and every moment is an expression of the divine flowing through you and for you. When you make time to become aware of this incredible presence in your life, you strengthen your capacity to love and to feel loved.

3. **I let go of the need to control:** I was scrambling for safety, and my anxiety was always dictating whether or not I would venture out of my comfort zone. Now I remind myself that the Universe or God has my best interests at heart and will always take care of me in my times of need.

4. **I became a safe space for myself and others:** I used to be terrible at keeping secrets. I mean terrible in every sense of the word. Passing them on to others was how I would feed my addiction to drama. However, if I told a secret to someone and they told someone else, then that was the ultimate betrayal of my trust. The rules were as follows: do as I say, but not as I do. As I began my healing journey of building my levels of self-esteem, I began to view myself as a sacred container and not a leaky bucket. I wanted to be trusted, and I wanted to also feel comfortable trusting others as well. Becoming so emotionally raw with myself meant that anywhere that I wasn't showing up in full integrity felt uncomfortable, so I vowed that my word is my bond. So if you tell me a secret, I am now an impenetrable fortress. *I promise.*

5. **I began to Be the Love in most (not all) situations:** We're human, and it's impossible to walk through life and not make mistakes. The truth is that when I started really showing up for myself on a whole new and loving level, reality began to bend around me. It's time to stop doubting your worthiness and start creating a life worth celebrating. The only way to do this is to Be the Love.

JOURNAL PROMPTS: Be the Love and Trust That Everything Is Energy

FEEL: How do you feel when you check into what your body is telling you right now in this moment? What are three things you are grateful for? What makes you feel in alignment with inspired and empowered energy?

_____

_____

_____

HEAL: What are ways that you can remember to raise your vibration on a daily basis? What are inspired actions you can take that will move the energy in your environment? What is your own specific gateway or stargate to connect with infinite wisdom and divine energy?

_____

_____

_____

REVEAL: What is your purpose in this world? How will you be of service to humanity and remember that you are a beautiful part of the human collective? What is your definition of love? How can you be the love and share it with others?

_____

_____

_____

8.

111 Self-Care Ideas to Be the Love

Here are 111 self-care ideas that will actively engage you in the process of being the love you wish to feel. When you learn how to take care of yourself, you will be able to show up in life and in relationships with more compassion, kindness, and authenticity.

1. Go to bed earlier so you can get the rest you need.
2. Commit a random act of kindness like buying a coffee for a stranger.
3. Treat yourself to a fresh bunch of flowers for your kitchen.
4. Take time to relax and enjoy a warm bath.
5. Create a vision board that is covered in words that represent your feelings.

6. Try something new like an exercise class or a cooking class.

7. Call an old friend and ask how they are doing.

8. Explore or study your family tree to understand your family lineage.

9. Learn about essential oils and how they can support your various emotions.

10. Keep a dream journal. Note down symbols, signs, and messages that appear to you in your dreams.

11. Paint a canvas with bright colors. You don't have to be artistic; watch how expressing your emotions in art form makes you feel.

12. Create a playlist of music that makes you want to move your body and feel happy.

13. Tell someone you love them.

14. Write a poem every day for seven days about how you feel.

15. Set an intention for something you want to manifest within a month.

16. Cook a delicious meal for yourself.

17. Declutter your closet and donate things you no longer need to charity.

18. Have a social media break, and unfollow people that don't inspire you.

19. Witness your predominant language patterns and note some of the ways you could be more loving with your words.

20. Creative expression: consider getting a tattoo of a tiny heart on your wrist (like I did) or even drawing a tiny heart on your wrist in pen.

21. Stand on the earth, dirt, sand, or grass in your bare feet.

22. Write the word *love* on a glass of water and then drink it.

23. Stare at yourself in the mirror and say, "I love you."

24. Go outside at night and look at the stars. Make a wish on one of them.

25. Drink herbal tea.

26. Commit to reading a new book each month to learn something new.

27. Write a letter to your future self.

28. Send a thank-you card to someone you love.

29. Watch a comedy that really makes you laugh a lot.

30. Support a cause that you feel passionate about, and tell your friends about it.

31. Create a time capsule with the things you love in it.

32. Buy some crayons, pencils, and a coloring book. Turn on your favorite music and color your heart out.

33. Burn sage or diffuse essential oils to clear the energy in your home.

34. Breathe deeply for five minutes.

35. Wash your face.

36. Give yourself a manicure.

37. Hug people or pets.

38. Do a crossword or a puzzle.

39. Commit to not complaining for an entire day.

40. Make love.

41. Try doing yoga every day for seven days.

42. Make a fruit salad with as many different colors as possible.

43. Read about a saint, mystic, or holy person from sometime in history.

44. Watch a documentary about nature or baby pandas.

45. Spend time staring at clouds.

46. Write out three wishes that you would like to manifest.

47. Create an altar or a space of inspiration in your house.

48. Learn a new language.

49. Make yourself a cake or a salad to celebrate the joy of being you.

50. Write a letter of forgiveness to someone that you would like to forgive.

51. Learn about the power of sacred geometry.

52. Light a candle and say a prayer.

53. Meditate.

54. Write the words *I AM WORTHY* on your bathroom mirror in lipstick or paint.

55. Give strangers compliments.

56. Offer to help someone without being asked.

57. Get really good at smiling.

58. Ask the Universe to send you a sign or a dream.

59. Learn a dance.

60. Go on a picnic.
61. Create a keepsake box to store all your special memories.
62. Create an herb garden, or grow something you can eat.
63. Plunge your body into really cold water for at least three minutes.
64. When you wake up in the morning, say, "Thank you for this day."
65. Make a piece of jewelry that reminds you of being worthy.
66. Color-code your bookshelf.
67. Buy yourself a small gift.
68. Remember to take your vitamins and your supplements.
69. Watch the sunrise.
70. Watch the sunset.
71. Learn about the phases of the moon.
72. Hug a tree.
73. Sleep naked.
74. Invest in nice underwear.
75. Clear out the clutter in your purse or your wallet.
76. Devote yourself to your journal practice each day.
77. Make a mandala out of flower petals.
78. Get curious about your spirit animals.
79. Learn how to say no and feel good about it.
80. Learn how to say yes and feel good about it.

81. Give yourself a scalp massage.
82. Learn about the chakras (energy centers) and how you can balance them out.
83. Get an energy healing.
84. Make up a song about yourself.
85. Read the love poetry of Rumi.
86. Raise awareness for causes that need your support.
87. Create a bucket list of things you would like to do this lifetime.
88. Learn a new skill like paddleboarding or knitting.
89. Visit a graveyard and send love to the departed souls.
90. Go to an art gallery and endeavor to understand the inspiration behind the art.
91. Read scripture or a holy book.
92. Ask for a miracle.
93. Visit a zoo or a farm and connect with the animals.
94. Stop making excuses for yourself.
95. Visit a candy store or an organic fruit market and buy something delicious.
96. Move your body.
97. Dress up as a fairy or a wizard and have a party.
98. Leave secret messages or money for strangers to find.
99. Be kind to yourself when you feel triggered emotionally.
100. Set clear boundaries in your relationships.
101. Stop and smell the roses. Inhale the gorgeous fragrance.
102. Admire the color of your eyes.

103. Find a role model or a mentor.

104. Create a seven-day meal plan.

105. Throw a dinner party, with wine.

106. Go roller skating.

107. Bounce on a trampoline.

108. Take a photo of a rainbow when you see one. Start collecting these photos.

109. Try to connect with a long-lost friend.

110. Design your own signature cocktail and learn how to make it.

111. Open your heart so you can allow the love to flow in and out freely throughout your life.

Afterword

Nourishment, Faith, Wisdom, and Compassion

The day after I completed the first draft for this book, I had left my office door open and a hummingbird flew in. I was trying to usher it out safely, but three times it perched on the edge of my computer, just staring at me. This was extremely surprising considering I had already written about two hummingbird encounters in chapter 2 of this book. Hummingbirds are known for being the fastest-moving bird creatures on the planet, and yet this new little friend was on the top right-hand corner of my screen just sitting there. I felt this was a beautiful sign of alignment for the beginning of the *Be the Love* book journey.

In the days leading up to finishing a round of final edits for this book, I experienced a dream that I have been having repeatedly over the last ten years. This might seem a little bit esoteric, but if you've followed me this far into the book, it should come as no surprise.

In the dream, I am aware of being a different person from a different time. I am a writer from the 1800s. I'm American, and I find myself in London, England, on a visit to my literary associate. I know it's London because I can see the well-known landmarks off in the distance—cathedral spires and bridges. There is a small village on the outskirts of the city with a row of shop fronts and a café that is only accessible by a rickety old flight of stairs at the back of the store. Only local writers, musicians, and artists know of its location.

In the dream, I hitch up my long skirt so I don't trip and am aware of being careful with each fragile step. Once I arrive down the stairs, there is a hidden café courtyard filled with familiar faces around me as I wait to meet with my associate for a cup of tea. I am working on a new book and trust that my literary friend will help me to find the right London publisher for my life's work.

One of the familiar faces is of an older woman with white hair, sitting three tables down. Her memories have faded, and her beloved companion takes her to the café to get her out of the house once or twice a week. In my latest dream, I spotted this woman eating a fresh slice of baked bread and enjoying every single bite, even though she couldn't tell you where she was or who she was. Every time I see this woman in the dream, she is a little different and a little less connected to the world around her as she fades into the energy of love. I feel sad to see this, yet compassionate at the same time.

Also in the courtyard is a private chapel and an incredible giant oak tree with magnificent roots that extend and burrow under the foundation of the church and the nearby buildings. In the dream, I feel at home and at peace. I am aware of how blessed I am to be a writer and a spiritual teacher for so many, and I feel a deep sense of gratitude for my readers.

Upon waking, I always ask myself, *Is this a past life dream? A deeply symbolic journey? A completely random subconscious adventure?*

When I woke up from this dream most recently, I felt an intuitive knowing of the potential meaning behind it and how it links in to the completion of this book—and also for my deep appreciation for you, the reader.

The awareness dawned on me in a new way.

The café represents nourishment—spiritual nourishment to be the love you wish to feel.

The chapel represents faith—connection with the Universe or a higher power and the source of love.

The tree represents wisdom—trust that you are the oracle and your intuition always serves you in your times of need. The roots of wisdom are the foundation for your support throughout life.

The woman represents compassion—that connection to other humans is the life force that makes being alive so wonderful. We're all in this together, connected by the energy of LOVE and Oneness.

And as for me, the main character in the dream (if it is me or an aspect of me), it reiterates that no matter who I am, who I have been, or who I will one day become, my work is to always share the Be the Love philosophy every step of the way to feel, heal, and reveal a path forward. I hope this philosophy will now be with you on your journey as well, and I deeply honor you for being here with me throughout this experience.

Gratitude

Eternal thanks to my husband, Sean Patrick Simpson. Life is so much better with you by my side. Thank you for your support, patience, unconditional love, and belief in me. I love you, always and forever.

Deep love and gratitude for you, the reader.

Special thanks and appreciation to my editor, Eileen Rothschild, and the incredible team at St. Martin's Essentials.

Thanks to the team at Piatkus, United Kingdom.

To my incredible agent, Jaidree Braddix at Park and Fine Literary management in New York. Thank you for your ongoing support and belief in my work.

Big love and thanks to my children: Thomas, Olivia, Lulu, and Ava. Thank you for choosing me to be your mother. Your presence in my life is my greatest joy.

Endless gratitude to my dearest friends, Dallyce Brisbin and Scott deMoulin. Words cannot express how grateful I am for your guidance and loving discernment over the years.

To Mark Joyner (founder of Simpleology.com), I am so thankful for your key insights, friendship, and wisdom.

To my parents, I love you both. Tony and Louise, thanks for having me. Henrietta—I am so honored to be your big sister. I love you to the moon and back.

Giant waves of gratitude to our amazing team at Soul Space Media, especially Jen Bro. To the listeners of the MANIFEST podcast, all of my manifesting students, and to all the people that read my articles or social media posts, thank you from the bottom of my heart. The collective energy of the community is what sparked the #BeTheLove movement.

To the hummingbird that was waiting on my computer, that flew in through the open door on the day after I completed the first round of the *Be the Love* manuscript. Thanks for showing up as a beautiful sign of completion.

Last but not least, to my ex-husband. Thank you for showing me that forgiveness is possible and that pain can turn into power. I am honored to have walked a difficult path with you to open up my heart to the Divine.

Next Steps

THE MANIFEST PODCAST

If you've enjoyed this book and you'd like to continue with your *Be the Love* journey, then subscribe to the MANIFEST podcast with Sarah Prout.

For more information, please visit
www.SarahProut.com/podcast.

Each episode will deliver you a brand new dose of inspiration in the form of an affirmation, a meditation, or an intuitive download from Sarah to remind you that you have the power to create your own reality. Let's connect with the Universe, activate the law of attraction, and manifest your dreams.

SARAH PROUT is a bestselling author, podcast host and manifestation mentor. Named a "Manifestation Guru" by *Cosmopolitan*, Sarah went from living on welfare as a single mother in Australia to running a successful seven-figure business in the United States. Over the past decade Sarah has inspired millions with her words on emotional empowerment, intuitive wisdom, and heart-based healing. She is driven by a belief that anyone can manifest the life of their wildest dreams and guide their destiny if they have the courage to do so. She is the co-founder of The Manifesting Academy alongside her husband, Sean Patrick Simpson. Born in New Zealand, raised in Australia, Sarah now lives in the United States with her family.